DS
107.4
.L313
1976

ISRAEL

Elaine Larsen

ISRAEL

Hastings House, Publishers
New York

First published 1976

© Elaine Larsen 1976

Made and printed in Great Britain

All rights reserved. No part of this publication may be reproduced, stored in a retrieval system, or transmitted, in any form or by any means, electronic, mechanical, photocopying, recording or otherwise, without the prior permission of the publishers.

Library of Congress Cataloging in Publication Data

Larsen, Elaine.
   Israel.

   1. Israel—Description and travel.   I. Title.
DS107.4.L313   1976   915.694'04'5   75-20480
ISBN 0-8038-3400-4

Contents

	List of plates	6
	Acknowledgments	7
	Map	8
1	The Land and the People	9
2	Israel Today	34
3	Jerusalem	49
4	Acre to Ashkelon	76
5	Judea and Samaria	94
6	Galilee	111
7	Tel Aviv	124
8	The Negev	141
9	The Borders	157
10	The Kibbutz	162
	Index	173

The Plates

1	Rabbi of ultra-orthodox sect, Jerusalem	17
2	Panorama of Jerusalem from the Mount of Olives	18
3	Jerusalem: Mea Shearim—the ultra-orthodox quarter	35
4	Jerusalem: soldier praying at the Western Wall	36
5	Acre: the mosque of Ahmed Jezzar Pasha	53
6	Acre: the sea walls from the south	54
7	Haifa: the Bahai temple	71
8	Druse shopkeeper and son in a village near Haifa	72
9	Roman ruins in Caesarea	89
10	Ashkelon: ancient water wheel in the ruins of Herod's palace	90
11	Donkey transport in Nazareth Bazaar	107
12	Bethlehem: the Church of the Nativity	108
13	Tel Aviv: Carmel Market	125
14	Costumes for *Purim* in the centre of Tel Aviv	126
15	The Dead Sea rift and the fortress of Massada	143
16	Bedouin children with fat-tailed sheep	144

Acknowledgments

Acknowledgments are due to Mrs L. Kaye who was responsible for parts of 'Acre to Ashkelon' and 'Galilee' and who was mainly responsible for the Kibbutz chapter.

I should like to thank the staff at Rex House for the helpful material they supplied me.

The author and publishers are grateful to the following for supplying photographs reproduced in this book: Douglas Dickins for plates 1, 7–11, 13, 15 and 16; A. F. Kersting for plates 2, 5, 6 and 12; and Peter Larsen for plates 3, 4 and 14.

1. The Land and the People

Two thousand years before Christ, the land between the Mediterranean and the Syrian Desert was known as Canaan. It derived its name from the traders of Phoenicia to the north (now Lebanon) where the famous purple dye, so prized throughout the ancient world, was produced; and the name was gradually extended to include all the inhabitants who were now called Canaanites regardless of their origins. Canaan was not a nation in the true sense. It was a collection of varied tribes and peoples, often wrangling and feuding with each other, and a collection of more or less self-governing city-states, each worshipping its own baal, or god.

The lively racial intermixture was in continual ferment as each group jostled another for a foothold. There were Amorite nomads who, tiring of the hardships of desert wandering, had moved into the coastal plain and settled down as farmers. (They were probably part of the cycle of desert nomads who settled to farm, and when agricultural land became more and more crowded and eventually less fertile, the poorest of the dispossessed farmers reverted to nomadic life again.) There were Phoenicians trading and sailing the coast from earliest times and Hittites and Assyrians in perpetual dog-fights for possession and conquest. Egypt, Canaan's powerful neighbour, was always a menace and her armies had already sailed or marched north leaving ruined cities, vassal-kings and garrisons of soldiers behind them. It was against this varicoloured background that yet another migrant tribe came to Canaan around

1600 BC from the Euphrates region to the east in Mesopotamia. They were called 'Ibrim' or Hebrews.

The story of the association of the Hebrews with the land, and their developing monotheism in contrast with the polytheistic cultures around them is told, of course, in the Old Testament.

Abraham and his kinsmen, as the Book of Genesis recounts, obeyed the Divine Word when they made their way to Canaan, thus demonstrating Abraham's faith in the One God. As a reward he received the Divine promise, 'Unto thy seed will I give this land'. For several generations the Hebrew people were to remain nomads in the region, with occasional ventures into Egypt when famine struck in Canaan. Abraham himself made his way together with his flocks and tribe down to the deserts in the south and his nephew Lot settled near the Dead Sea. Abraham passed through a number of the southern cities on the rim of the desert, Beersheba and Hebron among them. It is with Hebron where his tents were pitched that he is particularly associated. In Hebron also is the cave of Machpela, the ancient necropolis where he, his son Isaac and Isaac's son, Jacob, were buried. (A mosque stands over the cave now, for the Muslims too revere the Patriarchs.)

All this took place in the later period of the Bronze Age. Over the generations, the tribe grew and Jacob fathered 12 sons, themselves founders of the 12 tribes of Israel, according to the Bible. A favourite son, Joseph, made his way to Egypt and settled there, becoming a man of importance and wealth. The mysterious Hyksos shepherd-kings who ruled Egypt at this time were also Semites and their common origins may have played a part in Joseph's successful establishment, which enabled him to help his kinsmen when yet another famine in Canaan drove the Hebrews down to Egypt to settle in Goshen. The Pharaohs of the New Kingdom were less disposed to look kindly on the settlers however and over the years they were gradually reduced to poverty and serfdom, the 'yoke of bondage' which lasted for generations. Deliverance came through a rarely fortunate Hebrew princeling brought up at the royal court, whose name was Moses.

The Land and the People

Moses was one of those great figures that arrive from time to time and give their world a push in a new direction. His towering presence and spiritual authority brought a nation to belief in the One God. In the deserts of Sinai, the Israelites camped out until the members of the slave generation should have given way to the freeborn wanderers who would enter the Promised Land. The Book of Exodus tells of the historic events, including the giving of the Law to Moses, the Ten Commandments which were to become the heritage of Western civilisation for thousands of years first taught to the people whom he had led out of Egypt. The Exodus was a vast undertaking for large numbers of other slave peoples had left with the Israelites and shared both their freedom and their hardships. Acceptance of the One God and entry to the Promised Land was henceforth a goal of powerful spiritual unity. Even viewed solely in a secular context, it is still the dramatic story of a colony of slaves taking their first steps literally and symbolically towards the founding of a nation.

Moses, great teacher and prophet, died before the Israelites crossed the Jordan. His leadership had given them the spiritual impetus to bring them this far. Under his successor, Joshua, the business of settlement was to be undertaken. Many of the Canaanite cities were Egyptian vassals or held by its soldiers and the next few centuries were occupied in carving out a foothold among the quarrelsome rivalries of the land. To the sophisticated and wealthy cities, the invaders must have seemed uncouth and barbaric. Politically there was no close-knit structure—the tribes were independent and bound only by their common faith and resultant loyalty when trouble threatened. This was the age of 'Judges'—outstanding personalities who, for one reason or another, had acquired the right to lead or 'judge' their people. The reason was usually a successful foray against local enemies. The Israelites held their own in the constant battle for survival and the settlements gradually established themselves until, around 1200 BC, a far more serious threat arrived.

The Philistines, a war-like, sea-faring race, came down from the Greek Mediterranean, settled five cities on the coast of Canaan and embarked on a war of conquest. They were especially dangerous enemies due to one great advantage—they had weapons of iron. Their coming brought the Iron Age to a people who until now had known only bronze. The southern coast of Canaan where they established their cities, Gaza, Ashdod and Ashkelon among them, they renamed Philistia, or Palestine—which name, like Canaan before it, was gradually extended to the whole country and was to remain for three millenia. The third significant effect of the Philistine invasion was to unite the Israelites under a strong central leadership against them—the loose tribal federation, each tribe its own master, was no longer enough to combat their menace. The prophet Samuel frowned when the people came to him and demanded a king to rule over them—but the people had their way and the age of Judges gave way to the age of Kings, the constitutional monarchs of ancient Israel.

Saul, first of the kings of Israel, was anointed by Samuel about 1270 BC. He was a brilliant military leader, but he was a strange and complex man given to murderous outbursts of rage and fits of depression. By contrast, his protégé David was the nation's darling. His youthful victory over the Philistine Goliath had raised morale and made the shepherd-boy a national hero. The king's household was his home, the king's enemies were his defeated opponents. He had the king's daughter Michal to wife and the king's son Jonathan for his devoted companion. Finally and tragically Saul's jealousy turned against David, who fled the court and was an outcast in hiding when Saul and Jonathan were killed fighting the Philistines at Mount Gilboa.

Saul's death split the Kingdom in two, the southern tribes following David, the northern following the remaining son of Saul. On his assassination however, the northern tribes accepted David's rule, albeit reluctantly, and the kingdom became one. It was David who finally put an end to the Philistine menace and inaugurated the Golden Age of Israel. He made Jerusalem his capital and brought up to the city the Ark of the Law from Shiloh, a small shrine remaining as its dwelling-place until the Temple was built that would house it fittingly. The Israelites had always carried the Ark into battle with them and their war against the Philistines had perhaps been sharpened by the fact that the latter had once managed to carry off this most precious of their possessions. But now the Ark was in Jerusalem, and this one act established for ever the tie, both material and mystical, between the city and the children of Israel.

David ruled for 40 years and was succeeded by his son, Solomon. The country, which had begun to prosper under David's reforming hand, grew richer still under the capable administration of his son. Solomon's diplomacy and statesmanship provided the country with the peace it badly needed and consolidated the gains that David had made, (for by the end of his reign, David's rule extended from the Euphrates to the borders of Egypt). Treaties and trade alliances brought further wealth to a land which stood at the crossroads of the caravan routes in all directions; and from the Red Sea ports Phoenicians, those inveterate maritime merchants, and Israelites together sailed on trading missions throughout the Middle East.

Solomon's greatest building project was the Temple but he also built splendid palaces and fortified his cities—Hazor, Megiddo and Jerusalem. To pay for these vast programmes, he resorted to heavy taxation and forced labour which was bitterly resented. Solomon was far more of an Eastern monarch than his predecessors. His opulent despotism did not accord with the sturdily democratic character of his people—a character formed by the sharing of common hardships and dangers—and the northern tribes, in particular, were increasingly dissatisfied at the highhanded monarch from the southern tribes of Judah. On Solomon's death, the kingdom collapsed and the northern tribes seceded, forming the Kingdom of Israel under a rebel leader Jeroboam and establishing a new capital, Samaria. In the south, the royal house of David still governed the Kingdom of Judah in the person of Solomon's young son, Rehoboam.

Of the two, it was Judah with Jerusalem as its capital, that was to remain the channel of the nation's spiritual vitality. The history of the shorter-lived northern kingdom was one of bloodshed, inter-tribal feuds and intermittent peace. In 725 BC the Assyrians descended upon Samaria, laid it waste and carried off thousands of Israelites to slavery in other parts of the empire. Foreign expatriates who were resettled on their vacated lands mingled with the native populations to found the race called the Samaritans.

This was the age of the Prophets, although their role in the life of the nation was already an ancient and honourable one. Outstanding personalities would exert great moral force, influencing events so far as they could, in accordance with precepts of social justice and righteousness. They denounced the ever-present tendency to baal-worship and acted as guardians of the nation's faith and conscience, of sufficient stature to challenge even the king. Amos, Elijah, Hosea, Micah ascribed all the tribulations of the country at the hands of its enemies to retribution for the sins of the people. Exploitation of the poor, injustice, greed and corruption were the themes of their thundered chastisements and, regardless of safety or material position, they held fast to ideals in which humanity and justice were more important than mere observance of ritual. They were a major cohesive factor not only in the people's fierce determination to hold the Land against the constant threat of occupation, but in the survival of the Hebrews and their racial identity.

Nevertheless in political terms Judah was still an Assyrian vassal. The country was resentful and rebellious and, when Assyria appeared to be weakening and Nineveh fell to attacking rebels, Judah fought too under its ruler Josiah. He was defeated at Megiddo but the balance of power was shifting yet again. In 605 BC the might of Egypt was destroyed at the Euphrates, and that of Assyria almost immediately after as the Babylonian Empire rose to take their place. Judah became in turn a vassal of Nebuchadnezzar and the unceasing pursuit of its independence led to another revolt three years later. Although it failed and the king Jehoiachim exiled to Babylon, major reprisals were not forthcoming and the country enjoyed a measure of autonomy. But an attempt to form an alliance with Egypt brought Nebuchadnezzar again to the rebellious province to lay siege to Jerusalem. In 586 BC the walls were breached. The city was looted and fired and thousands of captives were forcibly exiled to Babylon, only the humblest peasants being allowed to remain.

The Exile was a major event though not a disastrous one. The people's morale and faith were still held together by the prophets, who were both teachers and leaders. Moreover, the Babylonian Exile was short. In 538, Babylon fell to the great founder of the Persian Empire, Cyrus, who in the same year issued his edict that all who wished could return to Jerusalem to rebuild the Temple. Some preferred to stay but it is said that over 40,000 returned. Later in that year of their return (and how quickly they must have made their choice and left Babylon) they gathered in Jerusalem to re-establish the Temple worship that was to continue for 400 years, and the rebuilding of the Temple was begun. This was hindered for a while by the Samaritans who had taken over land in Judah left by the Exile. Considering themselves kinsmen in faith—despite a good deal of idol-worship—they demanded a share in the rebuilding of the Temple.

The returned exiles refused, fearing a corruption of their renewed religious zeal and the Samaritans took their revenge by obstructing the work whenever possible. The Law was interpreted more strictly and intermarriage forbidden (it was at this time that the lovely Book of Ruth was written in protest). Ezra expounded the Law to the assembled people from a pulpit and the Temple, though central, was no longer indispensable to worship.

In 334, Alexander of Macedon marched through Asia and Persia fell before him. After his death, the empire so rapidly established broke up equally quickly leaving to the East the legacy of Hellenism. Ptolemy Soter, one of Alexander's generals who became king of Egypt, was now the new ruler of the country and first of the Ptolemaic dynasty. The influence of Greece was irresistibly pervasive and many of the Jews of Palestine adopted the new ways as readily as their neighbours. In Jaffa, as in other cities, coins were struck bearing the head of Alexander. Beth Shean in the north was renamed Scythopolis and a temple raised to Dionysos there. The Greek language was spoken widely, Greek names were taken. Alexandria was the centre of Greek influence in the area and vernacular literature was produced there by Jewish scholars and poets; later, the Bible in its so-called Septuagint version, was translated into Greek.

In 198, the Ptolemies were finally conquered by their rivals, the Seleucids under Antiochus the Great. But it was the reign of the other Antiochus (Epiphanes, or Illustrious) that gave an additional impetus to Hellenism. He was immensely proud of his Athenian birth and sought to make Jerusalem a city in the Greek mould. But while Alexandrian Jews might turn to the new fashions enthusiastically, Jerusalem was a different matter. There, the pious who kept rigidly to the letter of the Law were scandalized by priests who neglected their duties to attend the games, by naked athletes and gymnasts exercising in public. Worst of all, the Temple itself was desecrated by a statue of Olympian Jove which they were commanded to worship, and Jewish observance was prohibited.

Revolt was inevitable. It was led by an old man called Mattathias, a Hasmonean priest. With his five sons, he attacked a gathering met to raise a pagan altar, and fled to the hills of Judea. His followers, known as Hassidim or Pious, carried on sporadic guerila warfare and eventually established Judea's independence.

The Hasmonean era was to be the last period of Jewish independence until the modern State of Israel, and it was marred by continual unrest within the nation. In addition to the constant

1 Rabbi of ultra-orthodox sect, Jerusalem

Seleucid attacks, the attitudes of the Establishment were beginning to cause a rift between the people and their leaders. The priesthood was split by conflicts between the Sadducees (descendants of Zadok, the Hasmonean) and the Pharisees, more liberal in their outlook and interpretation of the Law. The people, too, resented the increasingly overbearing authority of the royal house and Hyrcanus' sons, despotic and rather unscupulous, did not help matters. Civil war broke out and though the fires were damped down somewhat during the reign of the aged Salome Alexandria, they flared up again with the rivalry between her sons until all squabbles were put to an end when Pompey marched into Jerusalem with his Roman legions behind him, in 76 BC.

With the conquest Hyrcanus, grandson of John, became a puppet ruler whose strings were pulled by Rome. Whatever power there was lay in the hands of his crafty adviser, Antipater, who took care to be on the winning side when Pompey was defeated by Caesar. Antipater's sons governed, respectively, Galilee and Jerusalem. Herod, governor of Galilee, flattered his Roman overlords (one of whom was Mark Antony) into presenting him with the tributary kingdom of Judea. With the help of Rome, Herod took the country and captured Jerusalem, allying himself (via marriage with Mariamne) with the Hasmonean dynasty to which he put an end. His reign was a mixture of cruelty, madness and capable administration. He murdered half his family in his periodic frenzies of jealousy and suspicion, yet put forward huge programmes of public works in Jerusalem and the rest of the country. He developed the ports, especially Caesarea, and built magnificent palaces. Above all, his pathological craving for security spurred him to the building of huge fortresses. In Jerusalem he raised the Antonia overlooking the Temple Mount, and the triple-towered citadel by the Jaffa Gate. He built the Herodium on an artificial hill south of Bethlehem

2 *Panorama of Jerusalem from the Mount of Olives*

and, on a towering rock overlooking the Dead Sea, he built the greatest fortress of them all, Masada.

After his death, Judea was even more firmly subordinated to Roman authority. Its ruler now bore the inferior title of Ethnarch, Roman garrisons were scattered throughout the country, the Roman taxes were heavy and the High Priesthood rigidly restrained. The land balanced uneasily between resentment and outright rebellion while the people looked longingly for deliverance, for the Messiah.

Around AD 25 Jesus was baptized in the Jordan by John, and began to preach in the synagogues of Galilee. In a land accustomed to prophets, he might have seemed just such another—ragged, uncompromising and versed in the Law. The people flocked to him and his first band of disciples, the fishermen on Lake Tiberias, grew very quickly to a vast following. But his teaching was unpopular. The imminence of the Heavenly Kingdom might be acceptable, but not submission to Rome and certainly not the fulfilment of Biblical prophecy in his coming (he claimed descent from the house of David whence the Messiah would come). Above all, his teachings could not supersede the Torah, the Law, as he claimed. The Sadducees were traditionally conservative in their orthodoxy and the Pharisees were embracing a more rigid piety in an effort to bring salvation the nearer. Another major force in the country, the Zealots, thought in terms of military resistance. His teachings were therefore unacceptable to those concerned with maintaining the national identity and overthrowing the occupying power. Barely three years after his appearance, he was arrested for blasphemy, accused by the priestly court of the Sanhedrin. He was tried before the Romans as a political criminal and sentenced to crucifixion, the hideous though usual punishment for runaway slaves, subversives and other 'trouble-makers'. To the Romans, it was a minor incident in a pattern of continuous revolt.

The Zealots now rose, fanatically determined to shake off Roman rule. By AD 65 Judea and Galilee were in open rebellion and riots broke out through the length and breadth of the country. Roman attempts at reprisals were staved off by the slaughter of 6000 legionaries at Beth Horon in AD 66 and Jerusalem knew independence euphorically for less than a year, before Vespasian came in Roman outrage to put down the resistance. The Zealots under their leader, John of Girschala, fought bitterly, and the struggle still raged fiercely when Nero died and Vespasian hurried to Rome to assert his own claims as Emperor in AD 70, leaving his son Titus to destroy the rebels. Jerusalem was besieged, the Zealots defending the city with desperate courage against appalling odds and holding out for several months before Titus finally smashed first the city and then the rebellion. Except, that is, for Masada, the last stronghold to give way to the brute power of the Roman legions.

Despite all this, the Jews of Palestine did not give up the struggle to free the country from Roman rule. With the Temple destroyed and the *Fiscus Judaicus* levied (the tax was originally a contribution towards the Temple upkeep, now made compulsory and diverted to Rome) Palestine was at best enjoying an uneasy quiet under the severe repressive measures of the authorities. In AD 132 another revolt broke out under the two outstanding men of their day, Simon bar Kochba and Rabbi Akiba, soldier-scholar, whose support and moral stature gave fresh heart to those who fought under bar Kochba's brilliant leadership. Again, a euphoric success was achieved, crowned by the recapture of Jerusalem. Three years later, against stubborn resistance, Hadrian put down the revolt with a ruthlessness exceptional even for Rome. Bar Kochba and Akiba were tortured and killed, and Hadrian's city, Aeolia Capitolina, was erected on the site of ruined Jerusalem. Jews were forbidden to enter the precincts and the great schools, the centres of Jewish intellectual and spiritual life, moved north to Tiberias in Galilee to organize the remnants of a decimated nation. Scholarship had always been important and it was held in especial reverence in these troubled centuries when the rabbis, or teachers, came into their own. Great scholars like Akiba, Hillel, Shammai, ben Zakkai, Gamaliel, were loved and respected by the people and accorded the moral leadership of the nation. In Mesopotamia, where an important community had existed since the Babylonian Exile, academies flourished and it was in these two major centres that the Talmud was brought into being, the vast compilations of rabbinical teachings on almost every subject under the sun and, above all, their interpretations of the Law and its moral and ethical applications.

By this time however, via the Edict of Milan in 313, Christianity had developed from a proscribed sect to the religion of the converted emperor, Constantine. Increasingly established though not yet secure, it regarded Judaism as a rival faith and took great pains—sometimes a little absurd—to prevent its being confused with the latter. As it grew in power, it resorted to persecution with only a brief respite during the reign of Julian the Apostate. The Byzantine Empire experienced a wave of religious zeal that swept the country and covered it with churches—Caesarea, Bethlehem, the Negev, Nazareth, Hebron, Shiloh being only a few of the towns where building went on. Jerusalem housed the great basilica of the Resurrection, the Anastasis, the Church of Eleona on the Mount of Olives, the Church of St John the Baptist. Monasteries were built in the desert where hermits and anchorites had made their dwellings in caves. (One example, Mar Saba, still stands in the Kidron Valley, amid the rocks of the Judean wilderness.)

The older religion was gradually being pushed out by the younger, and the Jews were now a minority in Palestine as the era of the Diaspora began to emerge. Diaspora, or Dispersal, was the Greek equivalent of the Hebrew word Galut, 'exile'. Galut applied to any country outside Palestine though dispersal had started long before. Slavery and deportation of captives was one cause, the travelling due to commercial enterprise another, and communities and settlements existed in many different parts of the Empire. Its northern boundaries lay in Europe and it was here that the Jewish experience was to be most significant over the succeeding centuries, both in the survival of a religious identity and in the conditions that brought about the return of the Jew to 'Eretz,' the Land.

The land itself was still a battleground in the seventh century AD as Byzantium, divided by theological rivalries and the numerous flourishing heresies of the time, fell to a new conqueror—the faith called Islam that had swept through the Arab world like fire. Its founder, Muhamed, was born in Mecca around AD 570 and it was there that he began preaching his simple doctrine based on belief in the One God and the evils of idolatry. It was really too bare to have much popular appeal and initially new adherents were gained slowly. Nevertheless, the Meccan authorities were hostile and in 622 Muhamed was forced to flee for refuge to the city later renamed Medina, literally 'the City' (of the Prophet). The Hegira, as the flight is called, took him in the direction of political as well as spiritual authority and his combination of the two gave Islam the impetus it needed to become the third great faith to arise in the Near East. Although, according to tradition, Muhamed was illiterate, he was familiar with the Bible—the Quran indeed draws heavily upon it—and he incorporated Jewish ritual and charitable precepts into the new religion. But the Jews were not interested in his attempts to convert them (their beliefs were already similar and they had prophets enough) while the Christians were totally opposed to him, being heavily occupied at the time with the theological aspects of Christian doctrine; and Muhamed gradually adopted a more hostile attitude towards them.

Barely a century after Muhamed's death in 632, Islam had spread across the East from Asia to the Atlantic. It was associated with conquests that came at astonishing speed. Of the Prophet's 'representatives', or caliphs the first, Abu Bakr, had marched against Syria. The second, the pious and tolerant Omar, entered Jerusalem. In one form or another, Islam was to rule Palestine with only brief exceptions until the present century.

Its immediate effect was naturally to subordinate the other two faiths, although the Muslim conquerors invariably showed a far greater tolerance to their subject peoples than the Christians ever did. The early rulers of Islam were of Bedouin stock, vigorous and simple and, although their faith was sincere they were practical rather than pietist in their outlook. (Islam was, in any case, as much a factor of political unification as a religious force and the Arab rulers were on the whole satisfied with the fact of conquest and its material benefits.) Payment of a heavy poll tax and a number of restrictions were considered sufficient and Jews and Christians, the 'peoples of the book', practised their religions in relative freedom.

Islam was now firmly established, though the vast riches of its empire gave rise to the old patterns of dissension and bloodshed. The enlightened Omar was assassinated in 644, as was his successor in 656 and *his* successor Ali, the son-in-law of the Prophet, in 660. Mu'awiya became the next caliph, founding the Ummayyad dynasty which ruled for a century before it was wiped out by the rival Abbassids (whose greatest caliph was the almost legendary Haroun-al-Rashid). The strife went on endlessly and by the tenth century, Palestine and Syria were in the hands of yet another master, the Fatimid dynasty of Egypt which claimed descent from the daughter of Muhamed. It ruled for less than a century before being overthrown by the Seljuks, the first of the Turkish dynasties that were to rule Palestine in place of the Arabs. The Seljuks were Turkish tribesmen from Central Asia and their harsh barbaric régime inflicted savage persecutions on the Jews and Christians alike.

By now however, Christendom was flexing its muscles. Feuds and famine in Europe were creating such unrest that a distraction was imperative. What better enterprise to promote Christian unity than to free the Holy Places from the Saracen? Tales of abuse of pilgrims and the defilement of churches in the Holy Land aroused Christian anger. Salvation and remission of sins were the rewards promised by the Church; and, though land-hungry nobles went for more material gains, the movement was fundamentally one of Christian idealism.

The Crusader era spread over two centuries. It was properly begun with the successful siege of Jerusalem in 1099 and ended with the fall of Acre to the Mameluke Turks in 1291. The first Crusaders coming from Normandy, France and Germany, knew no other system of government but the feudal and imposed this on the lands they conquered. Haifa, Caesarea, Jaffa, Hebron, Galilee, were all divided up into principalities and baronies, and handed out to vassals of the Crusader kings reigning in Jerusalem in return for their loyalty and the periodic service of their armies. This was at best an uncertain basis for retaining a standing army to defend and consolidate the Latin Kingdom, which was constantly under Muslim threat. In spite of this (and the slaughter of the local Jewish and Muslim inhabitants when Jerusalem was taken), Crusader rule was accepted by the local population and the country prospered. Local glass and textile industries flourished and trade improved. Under Baldwin, first king and second ruler of Jerusalem after Godfrey, the Mediterranean ports were secured, and a steady stream of pilgrims disembarked at Jaffa. To protect and care for them (the Christians at any rate), the religious military Orders of the Hospitallers and Templars were formed early in the twelfth century. The Italian states helped in the naval war against the Muslim fleet in return for trading concession for their merchants and these merchants established themselves along the coast, sailing to the West with silks, steel and spices, returning East with shiploads of velvet and pilgrims. By the middle of the twelfth century, the Crusader kingdom took in all the coast and reached over eastern Galilee, curving horn-shaped down to the Red Sea.

The Muslims, however, were still to be reckoned with. As long as their dissensions and savage rivalries balanced those of the Crusaders, the latter could hold on, but later in the century they began to inflict one defeat after another on the Christian armies, particularly under the great Kurdish warrior, Saladin. He had usurped the Egyptian throne (he was not an Arab) with the blessing of the caliph of Baghdad and, apart from the question of the

Faith, Palestine was of great strategic importance to him. In 1187, the Crusaders received a severe blow when Saladin defeated their armies at the Horns of Hattin and took Jerusalem. A third Crusade was mounted but was inconclusive and in 1192 Richard Lionheart made a truce with Saladin which allowed the Crusaders to visit Jerusalem, abandoned his campaign and returned to England. The Crusaders continued to rule their tottering kingdom from Acre, though in 1229 Jerusalem fell like a plum into the hands of Frederick II as a concession by its ruler al-Adil. The excommunicate Emperor crowned himself King of Jerusalem in the Church of the Holy Sepulchre—and left.

In 1244, Christian domination of the city was ended completely when a band of barbarian Turks, deserted mercenaries from Egypt, pillaged it and burned the Church of the Holy Sepulchre. The last Crusade four years later met with a limited success at a period when Islam was weakened by dynastic rivalries in Egypt, where the Mamelukes had risen to power; but five Christian strongholds fell in three years to the Mameluke Sultan, Baybars (among them Caesarea in 1265, Safad and Jaffa in 1268). Before the end of the century, the fortress of Acre was taken after a gallant and desperate struggle by its defenders—one of the few redeeming features of the final decades of the Kingdom.

The lions of Baybars face each other playfully on either side of the gate named after them on Jerusalem's east wall. Baybars was able, energetic and ruthless in war yet he was also a capable ruler who established the Mamelukes in the Holy Land. Their name means 'owned' and they were formerly military (as opposed to domestic) slaves of the sultans, converted to Islam. They had gradually become a warrior caste too powerful for their masters whom they eventually ousted. Fierce, turbulent and treacherous, they ruled Palestine for several centuries and, to an extent, administered the country surprisingly well. Communications were improved, benefitting Palestine with new roads and caravanserais were built to accommodate safely the European merchants travelling along the trade routes.

The Mamelukes were finally overthrown by the Ottoman Turks under Selim the Grim in 1516—a predictable outcome since the Ottomans fought with artillery against an army whose pride was its cavalry, trained from slave boyhood to the sword and despising firearms as beneath its honour. The Ottomans (of the house of Osman) ruled Palestine, Syria and Egypt for almost exactly 400 years until the Great War's consequences broke up their stagnant empire. They were much inferior to the Mamelukes although Palestine enjoyed stability and security for a time under their first, and probably best, rulers Selim and his son, the great Suleiman. Under their successors conditions soon deteriorated. The empire was too vast for any but the most capable and efficient administration. Instead, the pashas who governed the provincial regions were increasingly mercenary and corrupt, paying only a nominal allegiance to the weak and inefficient sultanate ruling in the relatively distant capital of Constantinople. Nor was Ottoman rule popular. The Jews of Palestine fared reasonably well (especially in contrast to their lot in Europe) but the Arabs, long since fallen from power, resented their Turkish masters and the Catholic Christians suffered constant harassment by the authorities who favoured the Greek Orthodox Church.

A notable incident took place in 1799, when the governor Ahmed Pasha (known as el-Jazzar, the 'Butcher') repelled a would-be invasion by Napoleon at Acre (with the British fleet lending its assistance); and it was partly as a result of the Napoleonic adventures in the Near East that the Holy Land became once more of importance to the countries of Europe. By the mid-eighteenth century, religious-political rivalries between the Western powers caused a spate of ecclesiastical building, mainly in Jerusalem. England, Italy, Germany, Austria, all established themselves there. France and Russia quarrelled—the former was the traditional protector of the Latin Kingdom in Jerusalem and Russia gave support to the Greek Orthodox. (The two religious factions had always wrangled over property rights and privileges in the Holy Power. Backed by political powers, the rivalry ignited a spark that led to the Crimean War after the silver star from the Church of the Nativity in Bethlehem had been removed by Orthodox monks.)

Consulates were also established by all the European powers, affording greater protection and security for foreign travellers and residents particularly in Jerusalem. A number of the smaller and weaker Christian sects of the east settled in the city and Jewish immigrants streamed in (increasingly those escaping from the anti-Semitism in Russia and Rumania).

By this time, the country was impoverished. For centuries its resources had been sapped by the endless wars and the heavy taxes. Its conquerors—Greeks, Romans, Arabs, Turks—had considered mainly its strategic importance, as part of an empire governed from Constantinople or Rome, Cairo or Baghdad. Moreover, the land itself had been neglected, a process begun as far back as Ummayyad times. It was natural for the caliphs to favour the Bedouin—but they were nomads, not farmers, and used the land for grazing rather than planting while the sedentary crop-growers tended to neglect agriculture under such insecure conditions and burdensome taxation. Under the Mamelukes, the system of government prevented non-Mamelukes (i.e. those who had not been slaves) taking office or receiving its rewards. This, in turn, prevented the foundation of hereditary estates, so no real attachment to the land could develop. By the fifteenth and sixteenth centuries, the trade centres lay elsewhere and the region's decline in importance was accelerated as Ottoman maladministration brought about a demoralized population, an exploited peasantry and a stagnant economy.

These were the conditions that faced the first Jewish settlers to arrive in Palestine on the wave of the movement known as Zionism. Jews had always made pilgrimages to Palestine and settlement, albeit in small or fragmented communities, had never quite ceased since Roman times in the face of considerable difficulties and hardships. They lived mainly in the centres of Safed or Jerusalem or Hebron, pious and poor, satisfied to be in the

Land. They were maintained by their co-religionists in the Diaspora and their days were spent in study and discussion of the Law, some of the greatest Jewish scholars in their midst.

Wretched and mean as their living conditions were, they fared on the whole better than Diaspora Jewry with its terrible experience of persecution. Hatred, bigotry and ignorance wore the same face all over Europe. In the fifteenth century, for example, when the Renaissance was occupied with its splendid new ideas about the dignity of man, The Jews were driven out of Austria, Sicily, Sardinia, Portugal, Lithuania and Rhodes. A French community in Toulouse was wiped out and Catholic Spain expelled or drove to conversion its population of nearly a quarter of a million Jews. The ghetto and the pogrom were the daily facts of Jewish existence. In 1648, when the Ukrainian Cossacks revolted under their infamous leader, Chmielnici, 100,000 Jews were tortured and killed in a decade. The horror seemed endless, the safe havens of peace and self-respect (of which England was one) seemed few.

The Jew's obstinate answer was to cling more tightly to the faith for which he suffered, and to pray for the Messianic coming and the return to Zion. This, in a sense, was spiritual Zionism although the term was as yet unknown. The idea took on political substance in the wake of the nationalist movements that swept Europe in the middle of the nineteenth century. Fifty years before, the French Revolution had broken down the ghetto walls and the Jews, in the first flush of their own emancipation, threw themselves fervently into the revolutionary movements of the time. But an anti-Semitic reaction (especially in Russia where the pogroms were more virulent than ever), brought a more sober frame of mind.

In 1862, Moses Hess published *Rome and Jerusalem* and put forward the idea of a Jewish State. It was met with little interest but the later book of a Russian doctor, Leo Pinsker, made a deep impression. Called *Auto-Emancipation*, it proclaimed Pinsker's doubts (as a Russian Jew might well doubt) that emancipation and assimilation could really work and his belief in a national homeland as the only way to keep Jewish self-respect and dignity alive, even in the Diaspora. His book inspired the formation in 1882 of the lyrically-named Hoveve Zion, 'Lovers of Zion'. Its offshoot, the BILU set out for Palestine to settle in small farming communities on the land: Rishon-le-Zion (First to Zion), Rosh Pinna, Zikron Yakov and Gedera. The name BILU was formed from the initials (in Hebrew) of the resounding call, 'House of Jacob, come let us go!'—symbolic of the moral fervour and the idealism of these early groups of young pioneers. In fact, settlements had already preceded them. Petah Tikva, the present-day flourishing town whose name means Gate of Hope, had already been established some years before, and the agricultural school of Mikve Israel before that again.

These were the beginnings. In Europe, a young Viennese journalist called Theodor Herzl was covering the notorious Dreyfus trial as a correspondent. Although a completely assimilated Jew, he was profoundly shocked at the anti-semitic bias that revealed itself and he decided that the only answer was an independent Jewish state, providing a haven from persecution for those Jews who found life intolerable elsewhere. His impact on the Jewish masses was tremendous, so much so that within a year he was able to convene the first Zionist Congress, which was held at Basle in 1897—the first major political step towards the ultimate goal of the Jewish State. Thereafter, Herzl made indefatigable and unceasing efforts—not always realistic, but always imbued with the vision of a Jewish nation—to focus the international spotlight on his cause, becoming its diplomatic representative in the capitals of Europe until his death in 1904. He is truly known as the founder of political Zionism.

In the meantime, the farming settlements increased as the settlers drained the swampland they had bought and fought the malarial mosquitoes. They established themselves slowly and precariously, learning to be farmers almost as they went along—and sometimes failing, as the appalling difficulties frustrated their painstaking labour. That they survived at all was in large measure due to the technical and financial assistance of Baron Edmond de Rothschild. But survive they did. By the time the Second Aliyah (wave of immigration) arrived in 1909, they were able to frown on the First for hiring Arab labour. The new arrivals, urban intellectuals, believed that Jews should be able to do every kind of work, including the hardest and most menial, themselves. The principles were those of socialist equality, self-reliance and the moral imperative to redeem the land by their own labour—a labour of love in a very real sense.

The Zionist leadership had now been taken over by Chaim Weizmann (later first President of Israel) and the Great War was being fought in the Near East as well as in Europe. Both Jews and Arabs participated, the former in the Allied Armies (they also formed their own battalion, the Zion Mule Corps), the latter making sporadic raids in the desert under T. E. Lawrence, to disrupt the war efforts of their hated overlords, the Turks.

In 1917, the cautiously-worded Balfour Declaration was issued by the British Government '... (viewing) with favour a national home for the Jewish people in Palestine'. Its wording left room for differing interpretations that were to have tragic consequences later on. Moreover, pledges had also been given to the Arabs, who fought in the Hejaz solely to throw off, if they could, the Turkish yoke. The two aims—that of a Jewish homeland and an Arab state—were not incompatible. Long before the war, Arab dignitaries had met Jewish leaders—Herzl among them —with mutual goodwill. (To the idealistic pioneers, the idea of an ethnic kinship dating from Biblical times was a pleasant one, and they fully believed in the benefits that would flow from mutual co-operation.) But in the main, Arab nationalism was hostile to its Jewish counterpart.

Having promised territorial independence to two nations (or at least a helping hand towards it), Britain emerged from the Peace Conference administering Palestine herself, under a League of Nations mandate. The Sykes-Picot Agreement, dividing 'spheres of influence' between the victorious Allies, was made public in 1917 (by Russia) and greatly incensed the Arabs. In the climate of resentment, they saw Jewish settlement as merely another threat (despite the fact that even as late as 1933, Jews made up less than 10 per cent of the population). In 1921, a violent nationalist, Haj Amin Husseini, was chosen as Mufti of Jerusalem—ironically enough by a Jewish High Commissioner, Sir Herbert Samuel. Instigating anti-Jewish riots, fomenting hatred, he hastened the deterioration of an already confused and uneasy situation, becoming a Nazi collaborator during the Second World War. The spread of Nazism was beginning to swell the tide of immigration and 'spontaneous' rioting increased, reaching a pitch of frenzy in 1936 although the British managed to keep control. At the outbreak of war, in spite of distressing restrictions on immigration and the increasingly anti-Zionist attitudes of the British Government, Palestinian Jews fought both in Europe and North Africa. Trained as shock troops against Rommel's army, Palestinian soldiers later formed the nucleus of the Haganah—the Defence Forces of the new-born State.

The end of the war revealed the horror of the German atrocities. To the Jews of Palestine, the rescue of the human remnants of the holocaust was a duty overriding all others. The British Foreign Office, to its shame, refused to lift the restrictions on immigration, making the infamous decision to intern the refugees of the Nazi camps in yet another camp established on Cyprus. Nor did the rest of the world open its doors to the survivors. Desperate with anger and frustration, the Jewish population clashed with the British military. The Aliyah Beth, the 'illegal' immigration of the refugees, ran the British blockade. Extremist groups, the Irgun and the Stern Group, embarked on terrorist activities in an attempt to break the deadlock. The Foreign Minister, Ernest Bevin, sought to delay positive action and exacerbated the situation still further, until matters were totally out of Britain's control.

Caught between conflicting promises which, in any case, she

could not fulfil, Britain finally threw the whole problem open to a special international commission. Its recommendations—that Palestine should be partitioned and autonomous Arab and Jewish states should be established—was passed by the General Assembly on 29 November 1947. Under its terms, the Jews were given limited territory, including eastern Galilee, the Jezreel Valley, the Negev Desert and part of the coastal plain. They accepted unconditionally even though Jerusalem was withheld. The Arabs refused to accept the UN decision and war broke out while the British withdrew, leaving their equipment and bases to the Arabs. On 15 May 1948, the mandate was formally ended and the State to be called Israel began its existence, the territories voted to it by the UN having been taken by force of arms in the months of British withdrawl.

2. Israel Today

Having begun its existence on 15 May 1948, the fledgling country took stock of all those things that any self-respecting independent state should possess. Did it lack a recent history? It had a venerable and proud past. Did it have a language? Over the last half-century, its ancient tongue had been lovingly revised and was now brought up to date to cope with the vocabulary of the space age. Did it need a sizable population? The immigrants poured in from 102 countries from every part of the world. By the time it acquired its very own Hilton in 1965, Israel had fought—and survived—two wars, had held seven national elections to the Knesset, its parliament, founded Tel Aviv University and had expanded its population to 2,500,000.

The contrasts were—and are—bewildering. The Land of the Bible was also the land of the multi-storey Hiltons and Sheratons, the de luxe Impalas would pass a laden donkey-cart: Bedouin nomads mingled in the souk with professors from Western universities and Christian pilgrims: priceless treasure of archaeology would be lovingly displayed, not only in the gleaming modern museums but also in a kibbutznik's hut. This the tourist sees—it is part of the attraction of the Land. But there are other, deeper contrasts which make up the picture of a nation in transition; and while the older pioneer generation fondly remembers

3 *Jerusalem: Mea Shearim—the ultra-orthodox quarter*

JEWISH DAUGHTER
THE TORAH OBLIGATES YOU
DRESS WITH MODESTY
WE DO NOT TOLERATE
PEOPLE PASSING
HROUGH OUR STREETS
IMMODESTLY DRESSED
COMMITTEE FOR GUARDING MODESTY
בת ישראל!
התורה מחייבת אותך
ללבוש תלבושת צנועה
אין אנו סובלים
שברחובותינו תעבורנה
בתלבושת
בלתי צנועה
אידישע טאכטער
די תורה
פארפליכטעט דיך
צו גייען צניעותדיג
געקליידעט.

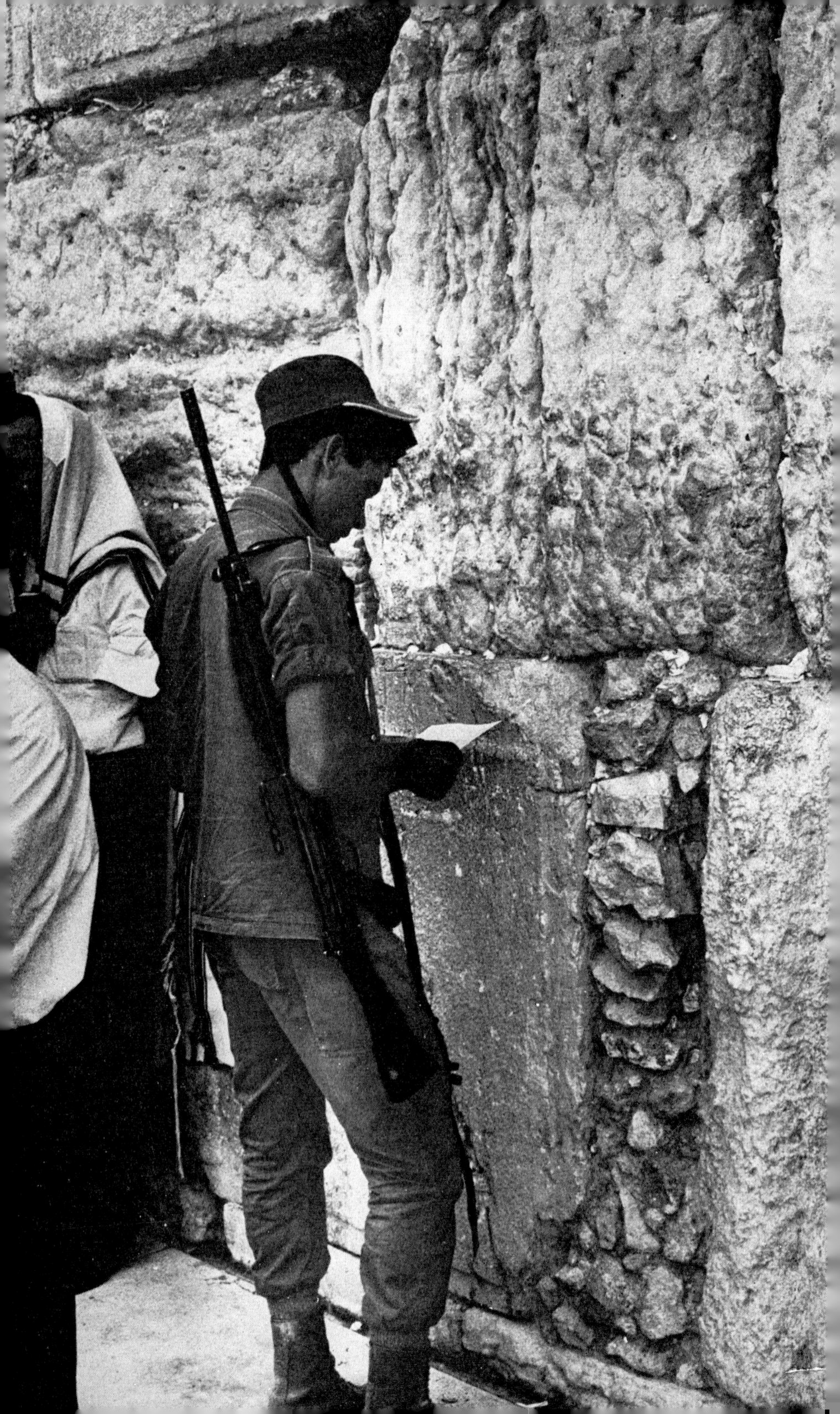

offering one tomato as a special delicacy to an honoured guest, young Israelis are already impatient with the stresses and strains bequeathed them by the accidents of history.

Initially, the sheer magnitude of the immigration might have overwhelmed the country. The greatest wave came just after Independence, between 1948 and 1951 when three-quarters of a million 'olim' (immigrants) doubled Israel's population. From Arab countries, such as Libya, Yemen and Iraq, Jewish refugees came almost in entire communities, ending a Jewish presence that in some cases had existed for thousands of years. The Holocaust's survivors—pitifully few—arrived from Bulgaria, Poland and Czechoslovakia. Most were destitute and temporary encampments, known as ma'barot, were their immediate homes. There were shortages of all kinds—money, food, clothing, housing, among them—but, somehow, the new Israelis settled in and made a place in this strange new society. The State of Israel was in business and the Law of Return gave legal sanction to the inalienable right of any Jew who wished, to come to Israel and be accorded full citizenship. (It was this law that gave rise to the unfounded fears that all the Jews in the world would immediately flock to Israel, spilling over its tiny borders to elbow out the other races living in the area. In fact this did not happen, nor is it likely to since Israel and the Diaspora each have their own role. Though often interdependent, they are individual entities and the majority of Diaspora Jews are content to remain that way.)

Over the years, the process of absorption has been streamlined and new olim find far less of the difficulties of their predecessors. But cultural integration was, and still is, a basic problem—understandably, in view of the great differences of origins. This has given rise to what is called in Israel, the 'cultural gap'—mainly between eastern Jews from a traditional society, often ill-educated and extremely poor, and Jews from the West, imbued with the

4 *Jerusalem: soldier praying at the Western Wall*
c

values of a democratic and technologically advanced culture. This is one of the deeper conflicts in Israeli society and may yet prove a stumbling-block to its development. But it is the interplay of such conflicts that challenge any society to remain on its toes, vigorous and lively; and the 102 countries and cultures that have brought their contribution to Israel have also made its most colourful and brilliantly-patterned human mosaic.

It is a shifting mosaic however, responsive to the pressures from within and without. As a country, Israel has had to grow up extremely quickly if only to deal with the tremendous problems of starting a country, as it were, from scratch. There has been no opportunity for steady, leisurely development and slow changes. The difficulties that faced the Yishuv—the Jewish community in Palestine before the establishment of the State of Israel—tested its strength and resilience in one crisis after another. Its moral fibre was tough, but it is understandable that today's Israelis still manifest the insecurity experienced by their elders in those early days of statehood. In many ways, the situation is little changed— the problems that should be given full attention by a nation at peace must, instead, be fitted in somehow with the recurring emergencies of war, on average every five years. And of the finances so badly needed for development and improvement, over half must be spent on what is proportionately one of the highest defence budgets in the world.

The Israeli temperament finds this especially trying. Israelis have no use for militaristic attitudes. They have suffered too much in the past to value uniforms above individuals and their army is the most informal in the world. Strangely enough, this may be the reason they are such fierce and disciplined fighters. They are, above all, a citizen army, each man fighting for his home, his family, friends and country in a very personal way. Officers and men are often on a first-name basis and short of parades, there is no spit-and-polish smartness. The army is considered a necessary evil and, as the country is poor and must economize where possible, it plays an equally valuable role in peacetime. National service is compulsory for all medically fit men and women after the age of 18 and the army is a major factor in the educating and blending of young people of so many varied communities—in particular, the oriental and less advanced. These immigrants often have serious difficulties in adjusting to a modern society and run the risk of hardening into a 'deprived culture'. The army, therefore, is an important unifying influence, providing an environment where the polarized groups can get together with greater understanding and respect.

Defence, development and the absorption of immigrants make the biggest demands on Israel's purse. Its people are used to living in what seems to be a condition of perpetual economic crisis. The cost of food and housing, always high, has soared particularly since the 1973 war. Yet somehow the money is found for those cultural activities that every Israeli knows are essential. The concerts of the Israel Philharmonic Orchestra are consistently oversubscribed; theatres are eagerly patronized and their productions criticized fiercely and knowledgably; museums and art galleries abound. Nor are such activities confined to the cities. Talented kibbutzniks may be released from their duties to pursue their art, the kibbutzim may arrange exhibitions, musical performers make frequent tours around the country.

'None is poor save him that lacks knowledge', says the Talmud. Israel is, more than anything, a literate country, ranking second in the world both for the number of books it publishes in proportion to its population, and for the imports of foreign literature —hardly surprising in a land where a man may serve his customers in seven languages! Newspapers and periodicals appear in Hebrew, English, Bulgarian, Arabic, French, Ladino, German, Yiddish—among others—and reflect every shade of public opinion. Television was started in 1969 with programmes in Hebrew and Arabic (and bored Israeli viewers can always tune in to the Jordanian channels instead).

The traditional Jewish love of learning has become the Israeli passion for education. The foundations of the Hebrew University were laid 30 years before the State actually existed and the beginnings of the Technion date back even earlier, to 1912. Today, there are six universities throughout the country, in addition to the 'popular' universities and the adult education institutes. A 10-year education, from 5 to 15, is free and compulsory for all schoolchildren and, since one of the aims of the educational system is to eliminate the 'cultural gap' entirely, special schooling is arranged to raise the level of the eastern immigrant children from African and Asian countries. These children are likely to leave school earlier than usual, and great efforts are being made to halt this trend. Sympathy and understanding govern these attempts which include 'enrichment' syllabusses to help these children to appreciate wider cultural values, in music and in art, extra help with their schoolwork and special grants for testbooks.

In its educational values, Israel is still in many ways a pioneering society and its children, loved and cherished as they are, are early prepared for their role as builders of that society. The output of energy required of the average Israeli child is truly amazing. With their ancestral heritage all round them, their education takes place outside as well as in the classroom. Noisy, gregarious and inquisitive, their spare time is usually spent at a local youth club or one of the numerous youth movements, particularly if the sports facilities are good; and it is rare, even during school holidays, for Israeli parents to see their children a full day, so wide is the range of supervised activities.

The children come into their own at most of the festivals that mark the Jewish calendar. Passover at a kibbutz, for example, is delightful. The long tables down the communal dining-hall are covered with white cloths, with flowers and with the wine to be drunk during the service. (The wine is not there normally. Israelis are notorious non-drinkers and their reluctance to imbibe except as a religious duty on Shabbat and holydays is something of a standing joke.) All eyes are directed to the raised platform that serves as a stage, where miniature Hebrew slaves cock a snoot at a Pharaoh barely three foot high and embark, singing lustily, on the Exodus, behind a bearded toddling Moses. It is a happy festival, a celebration of freedom and, by tradition, the young take part in the ritual festivities too. Inevitably, Israel's present difficulties are compared with the sufferings of the Israelites in their bondage; and an Israeli joke, tinged with wrye Yiddish humour, goes, 'Why couldn't Moses have led his people a bit further—say, to Switzerland?'

Nor is Passover, or Pesach, the only festival of deliverance. Chanuka, at the year's end, is a seven-day feast of lights, celebrating the victorious Maccabees and the Re-Dedication of the Temple; and Purim, which comes in the early spring, is the most carefree of all. The merrymaking is uninhibited, a jubilant occasion for parties and carnival—the famous Purimspiel. Again, it is an occasion to dress up—this time in gold or silver crowns, for it is a royal story of how King Ahasuerus was persuaded by his much-loved and beautiful Jewish wife, Queen Esther, to save her people from the wicked plots and machinations of Haman, his nephew, who wished to destroy them. The details and subtleties of the tale, as told in the Book of Esther, have no place in the Purim celebration which makes of the characters heroes and heroines and wily villains of deepest dye. The carnival winds through the streets, with 'dreyers' (wooden rattles) clattering joyously, and children may knock at any door to demand—and get—small gifts of sweets and cakes, the most delectable of which are the tricorne pastries filled with honey and poppy seed known as *hamentaschen*, Haman's pockets.

More sombre is Remembrance Day when prayers are recited and torches lit throughout the country in memory of the mourned and honoured fallen in Israel's wars. At sunset, Remembrance Day is ushered out by a massive ceremony where further prayers are read, with a blast of bugles, and the national flag is raised from half-mast again. From then on, and for the next 24 hours, the country rejoices.

All pandemonium breaks out with the celebrations of Independence Day. Until recently, the day was marked by military parades with the principal march-past taking place in one or other of the major cities by rote. This practice is now replaced by more limited displays, usually at Army centres. For the main part Independence Day is now an unfettered national holiday, devoid of religious overtones, in which the whole population takes part—including the various minorities with the sole exception of the intransigent Neturei Karta, the ultra-orthodox Jewish sect which does not recognize the existence of the State, claiming that it is contrary to Biblical injunction.

Such an attitude is an extreme example perhaps, but it points up one of the serious problems of Israeli society—the rift between the secular and the religious. Involved in this too are the distinctions between a Jew and an Israeli, between the Diaspora and Israel. The country is recognized as the Jewish Homeland. Yet it was established by political means, by Zionists who thought in secular, rather than religious terms. On the other hand, Jewish sentiment and devotion over thousands of years of suffering decreed that Israel must be established here, and nowhere else in the world. Throughout the centuries of misery, Jewish generations had looked with fervour to the Land, had incorporated it into their faith and traditions, had returned to it. The most pious had settled in miserable poverty, content merely to be on the sacred soil and it was natural to feel that the founding of the modern state was an opportunity for religious and spiritual renewal, for organizing the country following the laws of the ancient faith that had held the people together, retaining their identity until the Return of the present day.

The renewed spiritual vitality is certainly there—it accounts for the Israelis' vigorous response mentioned earlier. It is also manifest in the general political awareness, in the belief in the intrinsic value of the individual, in the constant social improvements. The Israeli obsession with social justice comes straight from the prophets, their respect for wisdom and learning direct from the Jewish tradition that makes heroes of its great scholars. Such attitudes are Judaism's heritage and much of its strength; and they enrich equally the observant Jew, the assimilated or non-observant, and the secular-minded Israeli. It has been pointed out that, in the reportage of the Arab-Israeli conflicts, a note sometimes creeps in of expecting Israel to show an example, displaying 'higher standards' simply because of what she is. Much the same attitude, and even more emphatic, is evinced by many Diaspora Jews who regard Israel as somewhat of the same order as Samual Butler's clergyman, 'a kind of human Sunday' who should perforce be sinless to make up for their own shortcomings.

Israelis resent having this thrust upon them feeling, justifiably, that they have enough problems to contend with already. Their undeviating belief in religious freedom—their State after all was born partly from the lack of it—extends also to themselves. The religious parties are vociferous and powerful in the Knesset, the prime cause of the retention of laws which govern matters as varied and different as transport on Shabbat or the question of who is or is not a Jew. The religious integrity is to be admired and respected. Nevertheless, many Israelis are in the exasperating position of feeling themselves bound in matters they consider purely private by regulations in which they have no belief, observance of which should be the decision of the individual, not the policy of the State.

The matter of religious freedom paradoxically enough affects the Jews rather than the minority groups. They may have their own problems but State intervention is not one of them. Out of a population of almost 3,000,000, one-sixth is non-Jewish. Tolerance is absolute, the Israelis being more scrupulous in this respect than any other of the Land's rulers. Even in ancient times, the Hebrews were not, nor did they expect to be, the sole occupants of the kingdom. Today, Druze, Muslim and Christian citizens follow peacefully their own modes of worship, and their customs and patterns of life enrich the Israeli scene. There are also the splinter sects of Judaism, the Karaites and the Samaritans. They are fundamentalist, accepting only the authority of the Bible, though the Samaritans also recognize Joshua, the Karaites rejecting completely the whole mass of rabbinic tradition.

The Druze are a pleasant, friendly people, originally a breakaway sect of Islam. With a number of villages and a total population of 40,000, the Druze have official status as an autonomous religious community for the first time in local history. The Christian community is also small, numbering about 80,000 souls. Nevertheless, there are numerous denominations, thirty in all, of both the Eastern and Western Churches. The Muslims are the largest minority group, with some 350,000 members. In a delicate area where uneasiness might be expected, in fact there is none. Nearly 100 mosques are open for prayer and if there is any religious barrier, it comes rather from the neigbouring Arab countries who deny transit to their Israeli Muslim brethren to make the pilgrimage to Mecca.

The festivals of the three major religions and their divers sects follow one another at a bewildering pace. Christmas, Epiphany, the Eastern Christmas, the Armenian Christmas, the Druze festival of Nebi Shweib (when a pilgrimage is made to the tomb of Jethro, father-in-law of Moses) in the lower Galilee, Easter, Muhamed's birthday and Pentecost. This rich and varied religious life is noticeable most of all in Jerusalem. The pilgrims at the Western Wall, the bearded Armenian priests, the visiting nuns at the Holy Sepulchre, all are woven into the very texture of the city and its air is filled with the wail of the muezzin, calling the faithful to prayer; with the blare of the 'shofar', the ram's horn of Jewish ritual; with the clanging bells of churches.

The re-unification of Jerusalem was the greatest event since the establishment of the State itself. It took place less than 19 years after Independence, and almost 1900 years after the Roman destruction of AD 70

The 6-Day War of 1967 brought, in addition, vast tracts of territory under Israeli administration—the Golan Heights, the West Bank and the whole of Sinai—and nearly one million Arabs. The spoils of war perhaps; but it is not the least of the

Israelis' achievements that they attempted (and in great measure succeeded) in the words of the Talmud, 'to do justice and to love mercy'. Today, the regions are more prosperous and better served in the areas of health, education and welfare and, as far as is compatible with Israeli security, they are largely autonomous. Much financial assistance for essential services and development comes out of the State purse. But the problems that were created for the Israelis go beyond the administrative and financial. The victory inevitably increased the self-confidence of Israel, if only by the sheer fact of enhanced physical security. At the same time, the future of the territories was hotly debated. There were passionate arguments, outcries, denunciations. A large body of Israeli opinion believed it had a Messianic mission to fulfil; saw itself in the role of unifying the people of the region and fostering love and brotherhood, with Jew and Arab learning to accept one another and live in harmony, as equals. The war also brought them face to face with the Arab refugee problem and in the euphoric months that followed, many Israelis thought that the time was ripe for a joint effort to solve it. They saw their own long history of flight and rejection as analogous to the refugees' plight.

On the one hand, Israeli reasoning is simple. Had the Arabs living in Palestine accepted the United Nations decision on partition, there would have been no refugees. On the other hand, the fact that the Arabs themselves have an interest in perpetuating the problem does not soothe the Israeli conscience. The malaise was heightened by the fifth of Israel's wars, the October War of 1973. Israel has always demanded much of itself and now, its confidence badly shaken, it turned to an uneasy re-examination of its own directives. The war took the country by surprise and its unpreparedness dealt a blow to its trust in the national leadership; an atmosphere of gloom descended.

The Israelis are still subdued. Yet there are signs that the gloom is lifting, that the fabric is beginning to mend. Israelis learnt their resilience the hard way and their re-assessment of the future, though it may be less hopeful, may turn out more realistic—in Herzl's words, 'Nothing happens just as one fears or hopes'.

Although the expert's predictions and the national targets are certain to be affected by the inflationary effects of the 1973 war, they are still a goal to be reached. Peace, of course, is the primary target. A government forecast made prior to the war expected the population to rise to five million by 1992, including one million immigrants. Economic expansion may be slowed down but the same forecast expected that the Gross National Product would be doubled over the next 10 years and industrial exports trebled. These predictions are not so over-optimistic as they might sound. Economic expansion has always been rapid and the Israelis, with their expertise and ingenuity, are hard workers— as their particular brand of humour puts it, 'The Israeli is so lazy, he will build a house in three days so he can do nothing the other four'. Moreover, war always has the effect of uniting a society against its enemies; so with Israel, still barely a generation away from the belt-tightening shortages of the pioneer days. Present-day circumstances may be a little more prosaic—the first advances have already been made, after all—but there are still villages and townships developing, as Tel Aviv did, into major cities; and desolate tracts of land that, with hard and willing effort, can be reclaimed for farming. And although the younger Israelis get impatient with their elders' fond recollections, there are no indications that they will shirk the challenges themselves.

The compulsory conscription provides the 18-year old with an alternative to an army camp—that of working on or, better still establishing, a Nahal. These settlements are the peculiarly Israeli response to the need for defence and the need to build the border garrisons defending the land, that at the same time, they redeem and make fruitful. The day-to-day privations and laborious effort required to establish a farming settlement from nothing, with limited finances, are taken as a matter of course; and the young citizen-soldiers take a rifle in one hand and a plough in the other, and probably with a book in their pocket. For however constructive the two-year period of service, it is still regarded as an interruption, though an essential one. Many will stay on the Nahal afterwards but more will return to take up other occupations or continue their studies. In the coming decade, 120,000 students—three per cent of the predicted population—are expected to attend Israel's universities, and the educational and scientific expansion envisaged will depend on them.

It is a truism to say that Israel's strength resides in her people. The same is true of any nation, Israel merely a rather more dramatic example. And its achievements are easy to explain in terms of pride in new-found statehood, in the desire for a national identity seeking to prove itself to others. This view, accurate as far as it goes, is a limited one—other countries have also gained independence, have fought against tremendous odds for survival. Yet even its detractors admit that Israel is 'different', and to look closely at that difference is to come back to the people. For Israel is unique in one outstanding respect—its original settlers and, in large part, its present population, come from outside.

What continually brings them here? The great waves of immigration of the refugees from Europe and the Arab countries have abated. The pattern has changed over the years and the present olim are neither destitute nor unused to the conditions of the modern world. For some, like the Soviet Jews, it is still a matter of escape from repression and persecution. The Soviet opened its doors grudgingly in response to world pressure—the emigration visas, the emotional scenes at the arrival of the new immigrants from Russia or Georgia, the rapturous reception and the universal support given to the Panovs, were a triumph for human freedom everywhere. This much can be readily understood. But this does not explain the reasons for immigration from those countries where such conditions do not exist. A well-paid Canadian executive uproots his family, leaves his job and comes to work harder for less material reward. A British or European doctor, or professor, or university graduate comes to do the same thing. None of them has come to escape a lack of liberty or opportunity to practise his profession—or, indeed, his religion or anything else. The question must be asked, why? And the answer stems from the same causes, in a way, that bring the refugees from persecution.

Israel fulfils certain very basic human needs. Needs which may best be defined as spiritual and which the visionaries and founding fathers of the country intended it to fulfil. How this fulfilment has come about is still something of a mystery. Arrogance and bad manners are frequent charges, frequently justified. The pace is faster, the people more excitable and impatient than the Western visitor, at least, is accustomed to. The bureaucracy is overwhelming and has been known to cause hysterics by the frustrations it imposes. Some native-born Israelis are resentful of the grants and privileges extended by the government to encourage new arrivals. The newcomer trying to cope with all this is understandably bewildered and sometimes disillusioned by it. But this is the surface and once it is penetrated there is time to look around, to get the feel of Israel as it is. It is then that the country begins to exert its peculiar magic. There is an underlying sanity and peace that can only be experienced at first-hand, a special quality that is the country's own. It is something quite apart from the worries and tensions of day-to-day existence, the anxieties of war. Along with it goes an extra vitality, a kind of intensity, to life here. Israel is, above all, an exciting country and knowing Israel is rather like making a difficult but rewarding friend. It takes patience and goodwill but the gains are immeasurable and enduring. Even those who leave again find themselves unexpectedly enriched by the experience—though how it happens, they would be hard-put to describe. Understandably so, for Israel's contradictions are endless—a nation founded by exiles, a humble and patient Jewish spirit which bred a people not noted for either quality, a secular Zionism which brought about a truly spiritual rebirth. Yet, in its contradictions lie its charm. It cannot be experienced by proxy—one must go in person to meet it. And it leaves no-one untouched.

3. Jerusalem

For 50 centuries Jerusalem has stood, crowning the bleak hills of the Judean Desert. It is bounded to the east by the Kidron Valley and to the south by the Valley of Hinnom, the Gehenna of ill-fame where human sacrifice was made to the god Moloch in ancient times.

The Jewish sages wrote, 'Of ten measures of beauty that came into the world, nine were given to Jerusalem'. A pious Jew does not merely go to the city—he 'goes up' to Jerusalem. In the centuries of exile, he faced towards the city to pray and throughout the world, the synagogues were (and still are) oriented towards it. Each year, the Passover service ends with the words, '... Next year in Jerusalem'.

Its name derives from 'ir-salem', city of peace or perhaps city of Salem. The Moslems call it el-Kuds, 'the Holy', coming after Mecca and Medina in spiritual importance. To the Jews, it is the holiest of cities, Jerusalem the Golden, the sacred centre of the Land as well as its ancient capital. It first appeared in written history about 2000 BC as a Canaanite city in the polytheistic cultures of Assyria and Egypt; and in 1800 BC Abraham came to the city and was welcomed by Melchizedek.

It was one of the few cities of that time, in an area of semi-nomadic tribes and squabbling rival empires. From the north, the Hyksos came down and overwhelmed the Egyptians, being beaten by them in turn a century and a half later. Babylon was a thriving kingdom and vassal kings paid homage to Amenhotep. 'The king of Jerusalem' is mentioned in the Bible (Joshua, Ch. 10), but scholars agree that an enigmatic people, the Jebusites, held the city until the time of David.

Ten centuries before Christ was born, 'David took the stronghold of Zion; the same is the city of David', and made it the capital of Israel. The events that followed gave to Jerusalem its enduring spiritual importance. It was here that David brought up the Ark of the Lord, with gladness and sacrifice of oxen, and 'danced before the Lord with all his might'. It remained to construct a fitting shrine for the Ark and Solomon embarked on his greatest achievement when, in his early years as king, he '... began to build the house of the Lord'. From now on, Jerusalem was to be the capital of Israel, politically and spiritually; and if, through the dark centuries of exile and persecution that followed, it could not be the former, this made it all the more strongly the latter.

The Temple is described in minute detail through several chapters of the First Book of Kings. Tens of thousands of labourers and craftsmen were employed in its construction. Great blocks of stone were quarried, and fir and cedarwood were floated by sea from Lebanon. The interior walls were decorated with carvings and covered with gold. In the 'oracle' (the Holy of Holies), two cherubim spread their wings ten cubits across, the outer wings touching the walls, the inner wings each touching the other to overhang the Ark—a shrine that, housed in the costliest and most beautiful of buildings, was sombrely lit only by a single lamp and contained no rich and ornate image of a deity, only the awe of His Presence.

It was the greatest moment of the ancient kingdom of Israel. With Solomon's death in 922 BC the political status of Jerusalem declined, but its spiritual importance remained supreme. For 200 years after, its material fortunes varied under a succession of greater or lesser kings but its religious influence was strengthened by the thundered teachings of the prophets who, outspoken and fearless, set a standard of moral dignity that has come down through the ages.

But the kingdom was by now divided. The northern half was overrun by Assyria under Tiglath-Pileser, and its inhabitants exiled. The Assyrian conquest continued south into Judah and Jerusalem alone was untaken, miraculously withstanding a siege led by Sennacherib after he had conquered the other cities of Judah. The resistance of the people, both physical and spiritual, was led by the great prophet, Isaiah, and by the king, Hezekiah. The walls of the city were strengthened, the Temple purified. The people, exhorted and encouraged into renewed faith, took the deliverance of their city as a sign of Divine grace.

But a power struggle somewhat less than divine was taking place between rival empires. Assyria was on the decline and Jerusalem became a rebellious vassal city of the increasingly powerful Babylonian Empire, then at war with Egypt. Like Sennacherib before, Nebuchadnezzar of Babylon laid siege to the city and met with resistance from the inhabitants. But this time, the city fell. It was levelled and burnt and its people sent in captivity to Babylon. The Temple was destroyed, its treasures looted; and the exiles wept when they remembered Zion.

The Babylonian Exile, remembered for the destruction of the Temple of Solomon, lasted in fact less than 50 years. Babylon crumbled and a new empire rose—Persia, under the brilliant Cyrus. Unusually tolerant and enlightened, Cyrus respected the infinitely varied beliefs of his subjects. Under his proclamation and protection, the exiles who wished to return could do so to resettle their lands and rebuild the Temple. Coming back in poverty to a ruined city, this was their first task. Progress was slow, the difficulties increased by the death of Cyrus in 530. But by 515, the Temple was completed and re-dedicated.

Much remained to be done in the city and under two great men, Nehemiah and Ezra the Scribe, the restoration of Jerusalem took place. Its walls were rebuilt in 52 days, all the communities of Judah taking part. They were inspired by Nehemiah, who gave the city the stable political rule it needed. Ezra assembled priests and scholars to teach and explain the Torah, the Law, in the form practised during the exile.

Jerusalem now enjoyed a rare period of comparative peace. but in 198 BC the persistent Seleucids finally beat the Ptolemies and annexed Judah. The influence of Hellenism grew and with it, the strain of two opposing attitudes, pagan on the one hand and Jewish on the other. A clash was inevitable and finally occurred when Antiochus Epiphanes sought to impose the worship of the Greek gods upon the Jews.

Antiochus decreed that the Temple, dedicated to the One God, should be renamed in honour of the Olympian Zeus. Statues of the god were placed within the Sacred Precinct. The Scrolls of the Law were destroyed and the altar defiled with heathen rites. Sacrifices of swine were made (an unclean animal, according to the Law) and Jewish observance was prohibited. It was carried on secretly and, when discovered, was punished by death.

The outraged Jews rose in inevitable revolt. The names of leaders—Mattathias, his son, Judah the Maccabee ('the Hammer') and his brothers—ring proudly in Jewish history. The Seleucids were flung out of Jerusalem, the Temple cleansed and rededicated and the event commemorated in the annual festival of Hannukah, which is still celebrated today.

Jewish independence lasted for only 80 years or so. Another great empire arose extending its conquests, and in the year 63 BC Pompey overran Judah, breached the Temple walls and made Jerusalem a vassal of Rome. With the exception of a few years return to independence, the destinies of Palestine and Jerusalem were now governed by the Romans. Herod had himself crowned king of Judea by currying favour with Rome, and attempted to do the same with his Jewish subjects by rebuilding the Temple. Whether or not he succeeded, his vast building projects bear the mark of his undoubted talent for administration. In addition to

5   *Acre: the mosque of Ahmed Jezzar Pasha*

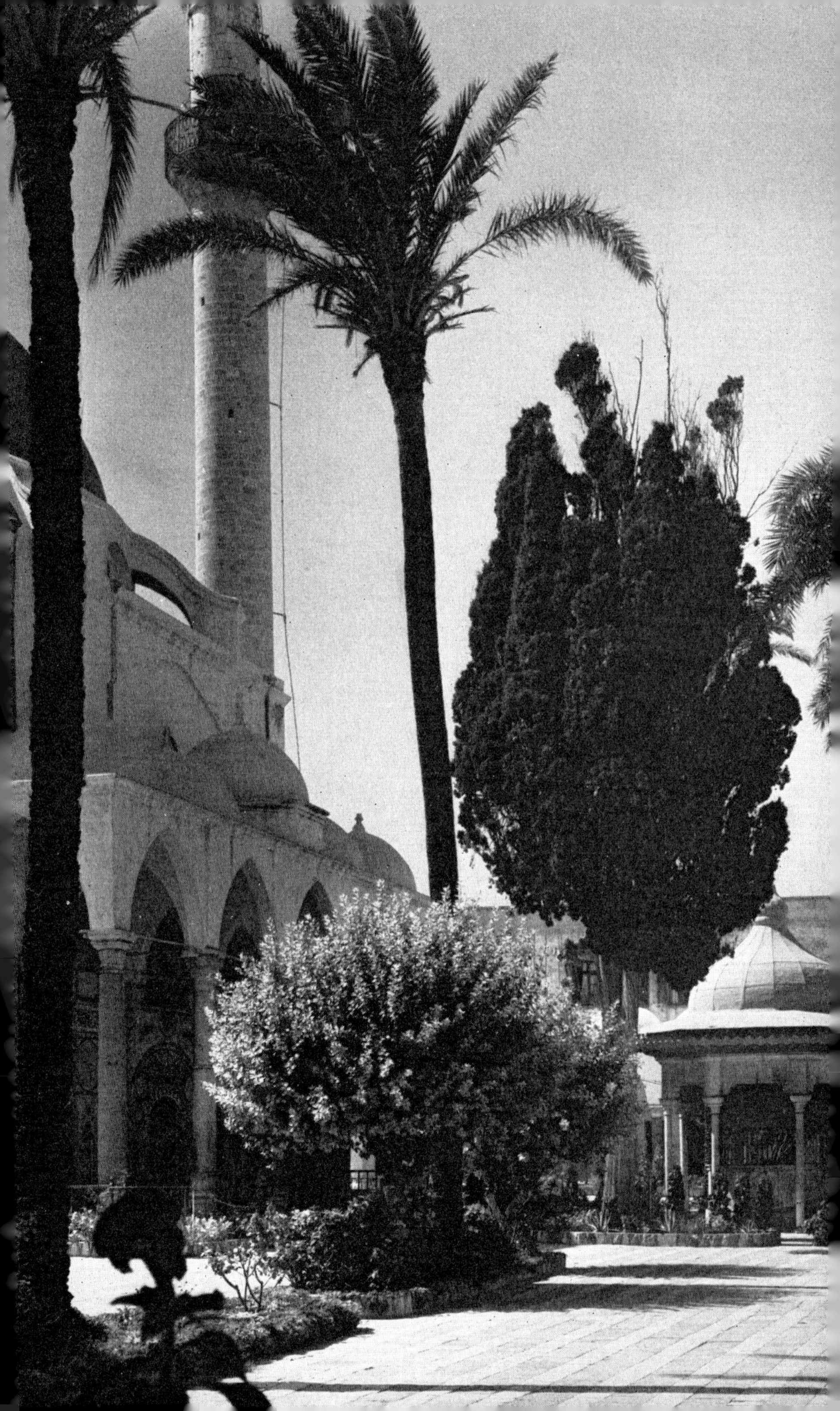

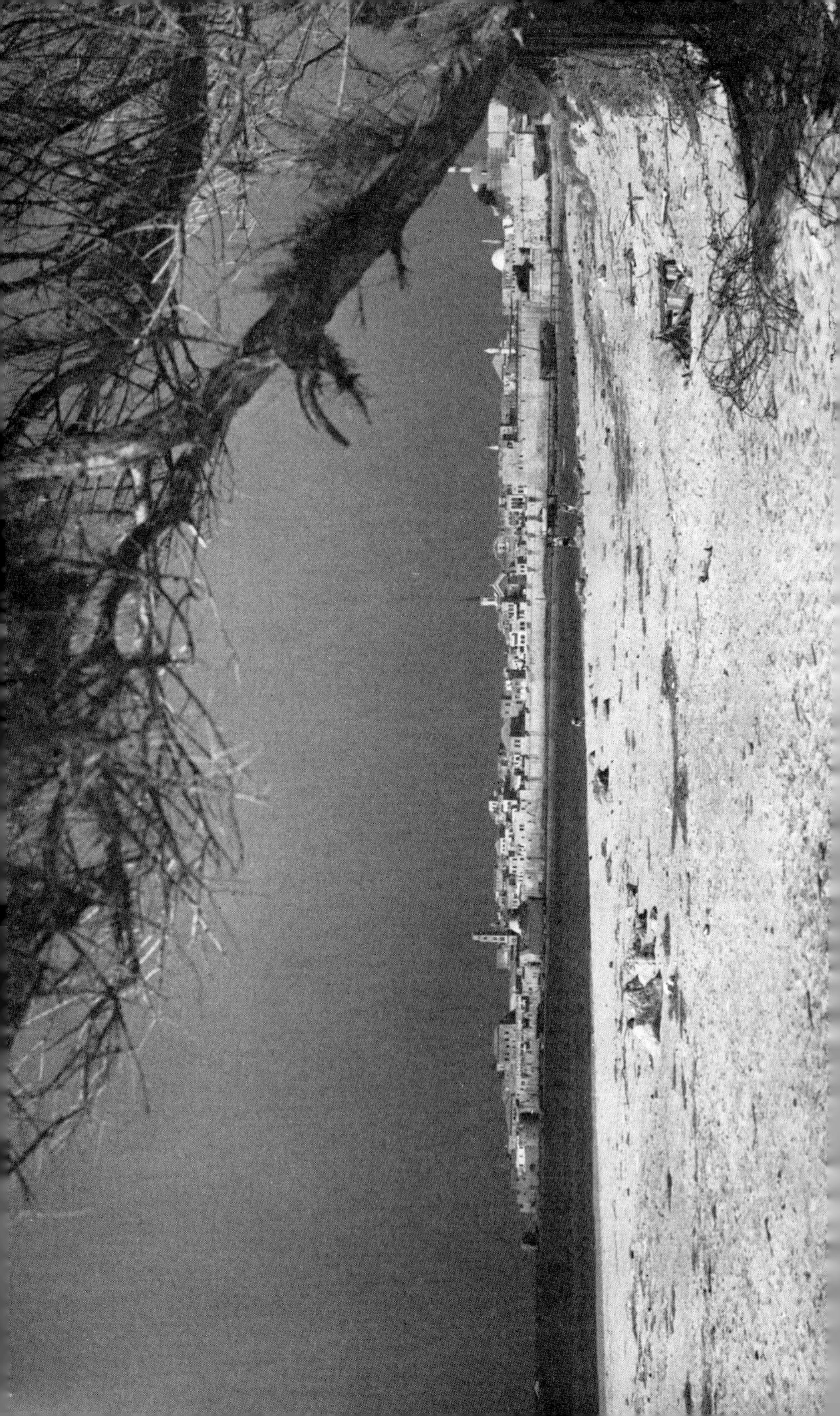

reconstructing the Temple (and it is the Western Wall of this building that still stands) he built fortresses and palaces throughout the country, his finest being the palace he built near the site of the Jaffa Gate today. Three great towers were the fortifications—the Hippicus, the Phasael and the Mariamne, named for his friend, his brother and his wife respectively. He also built the Antonia, the fortress at the north corner of the Temple Mount, over a more ancient fort called the Baris. From the Antonia, named in honour of Mark Anthony, Roman legionaries could watch the Temple for any sign of trouble from rebellious Jewish citizens gathered there. Despite all his works, Herod's memory has come down through the centuries as infamous (he caused many of his immediate relatives to be slaughtered including, in a fit of insane jealousy, his wife whom he had dearly loved).

While Rome tightened her grip on Judea, ruling it directly through 'procurators', Christ was born, an obscure Jewish prophet who preached subversively about a kingdom greater than Rome and a King more powerful than Caesar; and was crucified by the authorities in the interests of law and order. The old pattern remained constant—foreign occupation, repression and Jewish revolt—and this time ended in the destruction both of the Temple and of the city by Titus in AD 70. Sixty years later, the last attempt to liberate Jerusalem, under bar Kochba, was suppressed with brutal slaughter and the city was levelled. Its ground was ploughed over a new pagan city built in its place—Aelia Capitolina, after the emperor Hadrian (whose family name was Aelia) and the Capitoline Jupiter, the city god of Rome.

Rome however was on the decline. The Byzantine Empire rose and the Christians laid their claim to the city that was Jerusalem. In 335, Constantine built his basilica (later to be the Church of the Holy Sepulchre) surrounding the hill of Golgotha and the custom of Christian pilgrimage followed that of the Jewish. The emperor

6 *Acre: the sea walls from the south*

convert wished his Church of the Anastasis (Resurrection) to be the richest and most impressive Christian shrine in Jerusalem, and the architects of Constantinople, Zenobius and Eustathius, carried out that wish. The oblong hall of the basilica was known as the Martyrion. Spacious colonnaded aisles led to a court and a staircase approach to Golgotha, the site of crucifixion on a low skull-shaped hill ('Golgotha' is Hebrew for skull). Past this, the colonnades continued to the apse and the high altar. The great Rotunda of the Anastasis, supported by double rows of pillars, encircled the Holy Sepulchre itself, the tomb of Christ, carved out of the surrounding rock and enclosed in a small shrine.

The church stood as a place of pilgrimage until the Persians sacked Jerusalem and plundered it, nearly 300 years later. Later still, the heretic Egyptian calif, Hakim, was to destroy the Sepulchre completely, together with the shrine that enclosed it. At most, only the ground of the tomb now remains, as an object of pilgrims' devotion. In the meantime, the pendulum swung as the Byzantine armies conquered the Persians and brought back the True Cross, carried off as loot; and they regained Palestine, holding on to it briefly as Mohammed died and militant Islam marched through the gates of Jerusalem. In the year 638, the calif Omar was met on the Mount of Olives by Sophronius, the Jerusalem Patriarch, and conducted into the city.

Omar asked to be taken to the site of the Temple but the Patriarch, afraid that he might wish to restore the sacred place of the Jews, took him instead to the Church of the Holy Sepulchre. As the hour for prayer approached, Sophronius invited the calif to pray inside the church. Omar, refusing, explained that if he did so his followers might appropriate the church for a mosque; instead he prayed outside and a mosque was indeed raised in commemoration, the Omariyeh, which today stands south-west of the church.

In spite of Sophronius, the calif found the Temple Sacred Precinct and the great Rock, Stone of Paradise and foundation of the world. It was cluttered with filth, the Temple Mount being used as a refuse heap to inflict ignominy and Christian contempt upon the Jews. It is said that Omar cleared the rubble with his own hands; and the Mosque of Omar was built, a simple wooden structure in accordance with the austere piety of early Islam.

Over 40 years later, for reasons more political than pious, the Damascus calif Abdul-Malik built the Dome of the Rock in the same Byzantine tradition as Constantine's basilica. Enclosing Mt Moriah, an octagonal base supported the Dome. It was originally covered with gold and was protected by animal skins in inclement weather, but it was destroyed by earthquake in 1016 and, through successive caliphates, restoration was carried out in bronze aluminium and the exterior walls faced with glazed blue Persian tiles. The interior, with its mosaics and quotations from the Quran around the walls, its arches and pillars, dates from Abdul-Malik.

His son, Walid, ruling after him, built the El-Aksa mosque. Standing at the southern end of the Temple Mount (the Arabs call it the Haram Es-Sharif, the Noble Sanctuary) the silver-domed Al-Aksa was the true mosque of the Haram since the Dome of the Rock was raised not as a mosque but a shrine. The name means 'the Further Place of Worship', and derives from an interpretation of a surah in the Quran, although the 'place' referred to might also have meant Jerusalem or, indeed, Heaven. Little remains of the original building except a few pillars and it was much restored by successive Muslim rulers almost up to the present day when Farouk of Egypt donated ceilings to enrich its décor.

Muslim domination of Palestine (and therefore Jerusalem) continued over the centuries in spite of brief opposition from the Byzantine emperors. The califs ruled from Damascus and Baghdad and Egypt, with a degree of tolerance towards the 'peoples of the Book'—the Jews and the Christians, though charging them poll tax and extracting levies from pilgrims. In the final years of what was an uneasy balance (for freedom and tolerance depended very much upon individual rulers), the

Egyptian Hakim ran amok through Jerusalem, destroying synagogues and churches, and banning pilgrimages. The Church of the Holy Sepulchre was destroyed, although rebuilding took place after Hakim's death.

In the West however, a quarrelsome, energetic Christendom was looking east, greedy for profit and adventure but also urged on by its chivalrous ideals to the regaining of the Holy Places. One last invasion provided the impetus—that of the Seljuk Turks, who overran Baghdad, Syria and Palestine and captured Jerusalem. The califs managed to regain it for a short time but lost it again to the Seljuks who savagely persecuted the inhabitants, pillaged the city and banned or ill-treated pilgrims. Although the califs recovered the city briefly, the year 1099 saw the banners of the First Crusade outside Jerusalem's walls.

In mid-July, Tancred, Baldwin, Raymond of Toulouse and the Roberts of Normandy and Flanders, under Godfrey of Bouillon, took Jerusalem and entered the city, slaughtering both the Jewish and Moslem inhabitants. Godfrey was offered the 'crown' of Jerusalem and the title of king but, instead, preferred to be called Defender of the Holy Sepulchre and ruled the city under that name.

It was to protect the Christian pilgrims who now came, (though not Jewish ones, they being strictly banned from entering the city for most of the Crusader period) that the Order of the Knights Templar was formed in 1118. The soldier-monks, with their white red-crossed habits, took their name from the Temple where they made their headquarters, using the Dome of the Rock for their church. (The other great religious-military order, the Hospitallers, developed from a hostel for pilgrims in a small quarter south-east of the Church of the Holy Sepulchre which still bears its name—the Muristan or 'Hospital'.)

The Crusader occupation of Jerusalem lasted a little less than 100 years—but while it lasted, the city became once more the capital, instead of merely another city in a vassal province of whichever empire held power. The Crusaders built everywhere, as though to affirm their presence in the city. The Church of St Anne's is their work, and the Tomb of the Virgin Mary. St Anne's, thought to be the finest of the Crusader churches, stands in the north-east of the city, inside the Lion's Gate to the right. Its site is the birthplace of Mary and is where her parents were said to have lived. The Tomb is outside the same gate, on the other side of the Jericho Road in the Kidron Valley. It is cut into the earth and entered by a descending flight of stairs hung with lamps. It was here that Mary was believed to have ascended to heaven, and the Crusader shrine is a restoration of a Byzantine church of the fifth century.

They also built vaulted streets—if you walk through the souk, the market-place, you may buy your fruit under twelfth century archways in what was called the Street of Herbs, '. . . where they sell all the herbs, and all the fruits of the city . . .' And, most important of all, they rebuilt the Church of the Holy Sepulchre.

The entrance no longer lay in the east, where it had led through a court to the Martyrion and thence to the Rotonda. Instead, the church was entered from the south where now springs a cluster of chapels including, on the left, that of the Greek Orthodox St James and, to the right, the Armenian St John. In front lies the tomb of the Crusader, d'Aubigny, and past the divan of the Muslim caretakers, stands the Stone of Unction on which Jesus was anointed after being brought down from the cross. There is a legend that the skull of Adam is buried under Golgotha and buried nearby are the Crusader kings of Jerusalem, Godfrey and Baldwin. The Tomb of Joseph of Arimathea lies at the western end of the Rotunda and on the site of the Holy Sepulchre, two chapels stand—the Chapel of the Angel (that rolled away the stone from the Tomb) and the marble-lined remains of the Tomb itself.

The church interior is dim, half-lit, and here and there gleaming where the treasures of an altar reflect the candles. Ladders and scaffolding lend it an air of mundane untidiness (repairs are being carried out after an earthquake almost destroyed the church in

1927). Christian sects are numerous—and quarrelsome—here. Greek Orthodox, Roman Catholic, Armenian, Syrian Orthodox, Coptic and Abyssinian, all have chapels or oratories within the church and services are held by the different sects on a rota basis. Each guards its privileges and authority against the slightest infringement (frequently scandalous rivalries taking place over the centuries).

On the site of Calvary both the Latins and the Greek Orthodox have chapels. Set on the traditional place of the Crucifixion, the Greek altar is dazzling with frescoes, flowers, beaten silver, lamps and ornate candlesticks. By contrast the Roman Chapel seems almost austere, a restrained glimmer lighting a simple altar and a mosaic of a black-clad Virgin.

In 1187, Crusader Jerusalem was taken by the Kurdish leader, Saladin. Unlike Godfrey, he extended tolerance to the Jewish and Christian inhabitants and pilgrims and visitors of both faiths were allowed to enter the city freely. Richard the Lionheart entered into a treaty with Saladin (after failing to re-take the city) permitting Christian pilgrimage, and Jewish scholars came also, taking advantage of the new freedom. Less than 50 years later, political squabbles between the Damascus and Cairo rulers led to the city being 'given' back to Christendom—in the person of Frederick II—in return for a treaty of alliance; but after barely 20 years of Crusader re-establishment, Jerusalem fell to the Mamelukes who were to rule for nearly three centuries.

Although the general administration of the city was mediocre, Jerusalem did enjoy a measure of civil quiet. The Mamelukes were fairly tolerant rulers, though unimaginative, and Jewish scholars and pilgrims again found their way to the city—as they did whenever the foreign dominating powers did not prevent them. Christians also received far more toleration from the Mamelukes than the Crusaders had ever shown to either faith.

Understandably enough perhaps, the Mamelukes concentrated their energies on Muslim building. Churches were used as mosques (to rebuild a church required a permit), repairs were carried out on the El-Aksa and 'madrasahs' (combining mosque and school) were constructed. Civic works of general importance were also carried on and the city walls were rebuilt, as was the Citadel over the old fortress of Herod by the Jaffa Gate. Their distinctive red-and-white architecture still graces the Dome of the Rock complex.

But once again, an empire fell and another rose—this time the Ottoman Empire of the Turks, who met and defeated the Mameluke armies in 1517 and took Jerusalem as part of their conquest. The next years saw the reign of one of the greatest and most impressive overlords ever to rule Jerusalem—Suleiman, the Shadow of Allah on Earth, known in his capital, Constantinople, as the Lawgiver, and throughout his vast empire as the Magnificent, came to the throne as Sultan and kept a court that rivalled his namesake, Solomon, in glory.

Unlike the Mamelukes, Suleiman was a brilliant administrator, imaginative and efficient (as, with few exceptions, none of his successors was to be). Under his rule, the city prospered slightly and was enriched culturally by the Jewish scholars who made their pilgrimages and often settled. Christian pilgrims too were permitted again, and tolerance extended to both faiths in the best traditions of Islam. Despite a poll-tax, both Jews and Christians enjoyed a large measure of autonomy in their affairs.

Great programmes of public building were carried out. Besides the customary construction, repair and embellishment of mosques —especially the Dome of the Rock—the water supply system was extended and the walls of Jerusalem were raised in great rose-pink slabs of stone quarried from the surrounding hills to stand on the foundations laid by Herod. The Damascus Gate, the most impressive entrance into the Old City, was also built by Suleiman. It is an imposing structure, but its massive dimensions flanked by towers and tongued battlements are not for the repelling of armies and siege towers but mainly for decoration, a splendid piece of indulgence for the purpose of prestige.

After Suleiman's death, conditions sharply declined. The corruption that crept into the administration and the indifference of Constantinople—as long as the taxes were collected and the borders maintained—brought about a decay that continued under almost all his successors for nearly 400 years.

With the decay of civic administration went a decline in tolerance. Repressive measures were taken against the Jews living in the city, who were forbidden to enter the Sacred Precinct. Jewish worshippers, praying at the surviving wall of the Temple (the Kotel Ma'aravi, the Western Wall) and prohibited from the Temple Mount, would write their prayers on scraps of paper and thrust them into the Wall's crevices so that they could rise to Heaven from *inside* the Temple—and the custom persists to this day.

While Palestine sank into obscurity and apathy, conditions in the neglected countryside grew more and more dangerous with the breakdown of law and order. The walls of Jerusalem were the inhabitants' protection against the bandits that infested the surrounding hills and the ineffective garrisons of the slowly-toppling Turkish Empire would close the city gates at night, no-one venturing forth until they were opened again the following morning.

But in the mid-nineteenth century, a change began to be felt. The Jewish inhabitants were a majority inside the city and Jewish settlement outside the walls—despite its dangers—was beginning to be considered as a possibility by Jews living in other countries who, by their support, helped to maintain the Jews of Jerusalem (mainly a community of pious scholars).

In 1855, land rights outside the walls of Jerusalem were granted by the sultan to Sir Moses Montefiore, the Anglo-Jewish philanthropist. Weirdly enough, one of the first structures that he built was the famous landmark that bears his name—the windmill that stands (though damaged by Jordanian shellfire in 1948) south west of Mt Zion. More seriously, construction was begun on what was to become the quarter of Yemin Moshe, outside the walls to the west. However, another quarter called Nachlat Shiva was the first to be settled, followed in 1877 by Mea She'arim, the 'Hundred Gates' area of the ultra-orthodox and devout Jews from eastern Europe. The 'Lovers of Zion' were returning.

The great Powers also had their influence in Jerusalem. Russia, who of course gave its support to the Eastern Orthodox church, built a cathedral in a large compound, north west of the city walls and two years before the century ended, Germany made a grand entrance in the person of the Kaiser (for whom the wall near the Jaffa Gate had to be breached in order to let his carriage through). A Lutheran church, that of the Holy Redeemer, was built in the Muristan area, the Abbey of the Dormition—dedicated to the Sleep of the Virgin Mary—was raised on Mt Zion, and a hospital (now run by the Lutheran World Federation) was built and named Augusta Victoria, after the German Empress.

But it was to Britain that Jerusalem finally fell as the Turkish Empire crumbled to dust in the Great War. And it was Britain who, under the mandate, ruled Palestine with Jerusalem as its administrative centre, until the War of Independence in 1948.

During this period, Jerusalem experienced an upsurge of expansion and development. In particular, what was called the 'New City' grew apace to the west of the Old. The quarters so bravely begun outside the walls now formed part of the general settlement—residential and commercial—which flourished half-a-century later. With the immigration of Jewish settlers, not only the area west of the Old City was developed, but also the east. The foundation stone of the Hebrew University was laid in 1918 (by Chaim Weizmann, later 1st President of the Jewish State) on Mt Scopus, north of the Mount of Olives; and its inauguration followed in 1925. Also on Mt Scopus was built the Hadassah Hospital, and it was one of the most bitter of Israeli frustrations that, after 1948, both institutions were situated in unusable Israeli enclaves in Arab-held land, the Arabs refusing access to and from the sites.

The Israelis, however, made the best of a bad job and promptly started up the University in western Jerusalem—at first in scattered quarters here and there. The need for a permanent university complex led to the beginning of the new Hebrew University campus on Givat Ram in western Jerusalem, which by 1957 was a flourishing concern. Since the re-unification of the city in 1967, a new building programme for the Hebrew University is gradually transfiguring the outline of Mt Scopus. Haddassah Hospital also built a huge new complex beyond the village of Ein Kerem to the west of Jerusalem, a noteworthy feature of which is the small synagogue graced by the stained glass windows of Marc Chagall.

Near the Givat Ram campus of the Hebrew University is Hakiriya Ben Gurion, the complex of government buildings, with the Knesset, Israel's parliament, rising firm and square-set above. In front of the Knesset stands a large metal 'menorah' (the seven-branched candlestick of Jewish ritual and one of the symbols of the State depicting the history of the Jewish people) presented by Great Britain after the founding of the State.

At the foot of the valley facing the Knesset is the Monastery of the Cross, originally built in the sixth century and since restored countless times. At the top of the hill, facing the Knesset is the pride of the country's many museums, the Israel Museum. Its galleries shimmer with silver ritual ornaments and the embroidered dresses of oriental brides, and a synagogue of seventeenth-century Italy, brought over and lovingly reassembled stands entire. Grouped around terraces and fountains is a sculpture garden, an archeological museum and, possibly the most famous of all, the Shrine of the Book. Its white attenuated dome covers an interior expressly designed to harmonize with its most precious exhibit, the Dead Sea Scrolls of the vanished Qumran sect. Israel is a country of archaeological enthusiasts, its people eager to unearth and reaffirm their ancient links with the Land, and its history sits, sedate and orderly, under glass, to be treated with reverence.

Today, the pink stone apartment blocks advance further and further out and there are raw gashes in the hillsides where the next foundations will be laid for the new suburbs west and south.

Yet even at its most prosaic, Jerusalem retains an aura of special grace, not simply because of its religious associations.

It is a city of ever-changing levels and unexpected vistas. A road may rise imperceptibly and, through a sudden gap, the hills or deserts of Judea roll endlessly in the distance. The tempo of the city is slower than that of Tel Aviv and the atmosphere less raucous. Social life is a little more inhibited (at more than 2000 feet above sea-level, the cooler nights are less tempting to the outdoor cafe-lounging of Tel Aviv). The people too, though hospitable and friendly, are slightly more reserved—this is after all the Holy City. Yet, for that same reason, the inhabitants are more intensely and richly varied than anywhere else in Israel and the rhythm of the city is that of the religious calendars on the one hand and, on the other, the sound commercial instincts of its traders and merchants.

The inhabitants make use of progress, but keep it firmly in its place, tradition and custom being more important. In Mea Shearim, for instance, the life is still that of the ghettos of eighteenth-century Poland and the men defy Jerusalem's sun in the long black coats and heavy fur-trimmed 'streimels' of their ancestors. In obedience to the injunctions prominently displayed above the streets, the women (even the little girls) have their knees and elbows hidden, like the 'modest daughters of the Torah' they are taught to be. A mini-skirt may well be spat on with pious disgust and cars driven through the quarter after sunset on Friday profane the Sabbath and are stoned. Their religious bigotry is better understood in the light of the persecution endured over the centuries and becomes bravery when one realizes their stubborn clinging to the Faith meant even greater persecution. The most extreme of the orthodox sects, the Neturei Karta, refused indeed to recognize the State of Israel, believing it should have waited the Messiah's coming.

Once out of the district, the oppressive atmosphere of this admirable piety lightens, changing completely a few blocks away to the homely bustle of Machnei Yehuda, the most attractive market in Jerusalem. The man who sells bananas may also sell lottery tickets, the poultryman plucks his chickens in the street and brawny 'kosher' butchers stand with long sidelocks nodding over their vast striped aprons. It is a friendly place, if not quite as exotic as the Souk inside the Damascus Gate. It is a city of markets and not only from necessity. Much social life goes on here—the market is a place where friends are certain to meet, the cafés are a forum for gossip, the passing crowds a never-ending entertainment. On Friday mornings, the Bedouin come to the city to hold their livestock market under the east wall. Tourists, surprisingly, are not much in evidence though it's a picturesque affair with betasselled horses being put through their paces, and flocks of sheep and goats milling dustily about, herded by wives or small children while the men bargain and bicker enjoyably through the morning.

In the afternoon, Jerusalem remembers that it is a pilgrim city and the processions, organized by the Franciscans who also did much to promote the tradition, file up the Via Dolorosa, the Way of Sorrows, to visit the Stations of the Cross. An Arab boys' school now stands on the traditional site of the First Station, the courtyard of the Antonia where Jesus was sentenced by Pilate. The nearby paving stones, the Lithostrotos, still retain the marks made by bored Roman soldiers whiling away the time with games of dice.

Opposite, the Convent of the Flagellation and the Chapel of the Condemnation stand in the same complex, traditionally on the site of these events of the Passion. The Arch of Ecce Homo, 'Behold the Man', is the next Station. The pilgrims who came here in medieval times believed that Pilate uttered his words on this spot and the Arch kept the name and associations even after it was discovered that Hadrian built it in the second century AD as a gateway to his city, Aelia Capitolina. Our Lady of the Spasm, an Armenian church, marks the Fourth Station where Mary fainted on meeting Jesus; then the road mounts in shallow layered steps to Calvary. At the Seventh Station, Christ fell for the second time and the site is marked near the ancient course of the city walls.

The Eighth Station, marked by a cross in the wall of St Charalambos, is the last in the Via itself. The remaining five Stations of the pitiful journey lie inside the Church of the Holy Sepulchre. The Tenth, where Jesus was stripped, is the Latin chapel on Calvary and its altar is the Eleventh Station, where Jesus was nailed to the cross. The Twelfth Station is the Greek Orthodox chapel which shares Calvary, marking the raising of the cross and Jesus' death; the Stabat Mater nearby, the Thirteenth Station where his body was brought down from the cross; and his place of burial, the Fourteenth Station, the Holy Sepulchre.

This was the path followed by the Crusaders although, long before, a route since forgotten was trodden from Gethsemane to Calvary. Developed by pilgrimage, the Stations of the present route, like so many shrines in this city, are hallowed by time and belief in spite of the scholars' doubts or the findings of the archaeologists. At Easter the processions move densely through the narrow streets. Roman soldiers hurry round a corner to take their places while an elderly woman, from Italy perhaps, or Greece, struggles beneath a huge cross, her face contorted with effort and the thought of Christ's anguish.

Less harrowing, the Protestants—who have no chapel in the Holy Sepulchre—make their quieter visits to the Garden Tomb which lies outside the Damascus Gate along the Nablus Road (on the site that General Gordon thought to be Calvary although the evidence points to it being part of a necropolis from the time of Herod, and its authenticity is doubtful). Both Protestants and Catholics make their pilgrimage to the west of the city where the village of Ein Kerem clings to the wooded hillside, birthplace of John the Baptist. The meeting of Mary and the Baptist's mother, Elizabeth, is commemorated by the Church of the Visitation.

According to Christian belief, Christ ascended to heaven from the summit of the Mount of Olives, and in the fourth century two churches were built here. On the remains of one, a fine basilica of Constantine surpassed only by the Church of the Holy Sepulchre, now rises the Basilica of the Sacred Heart. The other was the small octagonal Chapel of the Ascension, built as a shrine and restored many times since. On Palm Sunday, the Catholics come in procession, following Christ's footsteps into Jerusalem from Bethphage, down the slopes of the Mount of Olives. The chapel of Dominus Flevit stands here to the left, its arched window framing the city over which Christ wept. Beyond is Gethsemane ('Gat-shemanim' is Hebrew for oil-press), where he kept vigil among the olive-trees before the journey that led to the cross. Czar Alexander III built an exotic, onion-domed church here and named it after his mother's patron saint, Mary Magdalene; but the shrine of Christ's agony is the basilica lying further down the slope. It was raised less than half a century ago, a bubble of domes behind a mosaic façade. So many countries contributed gifts to its building that it is now called the Church of All Nations.

But the significance of the Mount of Olives goes back long before Christ. Today, its Hebrew name is simply a translation of the English one but in ancient times its name meant 'Mount of Anointing', and in Jewish tradition it was here that the Messiah would first come, bringing the Resurrection. For centuries, it was the wish of devout Jews to be buried here that they might the sooner be resurrected, and their graves line the long slope south to the Kidron Valley. This most ancient and largest of Jewish cemeteries was desecrated when the Jordanians bulldozed a road through here, and used the tombstones for their army latrines, for pavements and for buildings, scattering the bones of the dead. Work goes on ceaselessly to identify and re-inter the remains, to find the tombstones and to restore and reconsecrate the grave-yard.

To the west, Gethsemane rises behind tombs more ancient still—Jehosophat's and Absalom's they are called, though they were built long after Biblical times. This is the northern tip of the Kidron Valley. At its southern end the City of David stood, a narrow strip watered by the Gihon spring at its east wall. (Beneath its foundations, Jerusalem is a maze of cisterns and conduits that watered the city from underground pools and ancient aqueducts, long disused.) Later, the northern boundary was extended by Solomon, and enclosed the Temple compound. Here, the walls are pierced by the Dung Gate where the city's rubbish was said to have been carried out (but it is intriguing to note that 'Solomon's Stables' are near here, underneath the Temple Mount. The Romans used them as did the Crusaders, whose carved mangers still remain).

Inside the walls at this point is the old Jewish Quarter. Its squat domed houses crowd densely around the ruins of the many synagogues—some first built in the Middle Ages—that once stood here and were destroyed prior to the 1967 war. Under the Israeli Government, they are now being restored, notably the largest, called the Hurva (its name means 'ruin'), blending modern architecture with the characteristic forms of the Old City to make a picturesque residential area.

Next door to it, stands the Armenian Quarter, quietly self-contained with black-clad monks appearing from the dim recesses of St James' church, their hoods fluttering behind them. They look as sinister as the Inquisition but are friendly and prosaic, and run a boys' school for fledgling priests.

The narrow street broadens here, bending to the left and changing its name to Omar ben Khattab to lead out of the Old City through the Jaffa Gate, leaving behind the crowded bazaar of David Street. The tower of the Citadel also bears David's name although the fortress was one of Herod's huge building projects. Its strategic value made it of major importance in the unending battles fought for Jerusalem. The Crusaders used it and after them, the Turks. Now, in reunited Jerusalem, the tower overlooks nothing more menacing than a bus station, and an artists' quarter has been established outside; the most dramatic incidents that happen here take place in the *son et lumière* performances given on summer evenings.

The city lives intensely behind its walls and the souks, or bazaars, are its commercial lifeline, David Street being a narrower tributary of the Khan el-Zeit, the major channel that courses exuberantly through the city from the Damascus Gate. The shops dazzle and bewitch, and the tawdriness and sameness of much of their merchandise becomes unimportant, either almost lost in the brilliant confusion or displayed indiscriminately with the fine craftsmanship of a dozen different regions. Plastic rosaries ('souvenirs from the Holy Land') hang alongside Bedouin necklets of coral and old coins; cheap miniature caravans—3 camels apiece—share a window with handblown jewel-coloured Hebron glass or gilt trays engraved with Arabic script or the marvellously delicate embroidery in gold and silver thread of the Yemenite Jews who brought their traditional crafts with them to Israel. A certain amount of haggling is permitted, just enough for tourist self-respect (a guide brought along for the purpose will take his cut probably, allowing for it in the price) but nevertheless, the market compares favourably with the shops for the price and variety of its exotica.

There are other delights too. The Arab restaurants, dubious to look at, serve surprisingly good food. Meats, vegetables and soups simmer in large vats and are served plentifully with flat 'pita' bread kept warm by the stove. In the Khan el-Zeit, you can eat an Arab lunch and buy a baba-au-rhum for dessert from the refrigerated counter of an Israeli pastry-shop a few yards away; or munch almonds; or olives; or grapes; or sesame seeds; or Arab sweets (bright green, sticky fondant or shredded sweet cakes dripping with honey); or English chocolate, sold at exorbitant prices inside the Damascus Gate.

At night, a more seemly tranquillity descends. The cafés of course are still open and there is *son et lumière* at the Citadel. But the crowds have gone and the life of the streets is now indoors. The great space before the Western Wall is unpeopled and soundless, although it is never quite deserted. Because the Wall is a synagogue, the head must be covered and men and women

7   *Haifa: the Bahai temple*

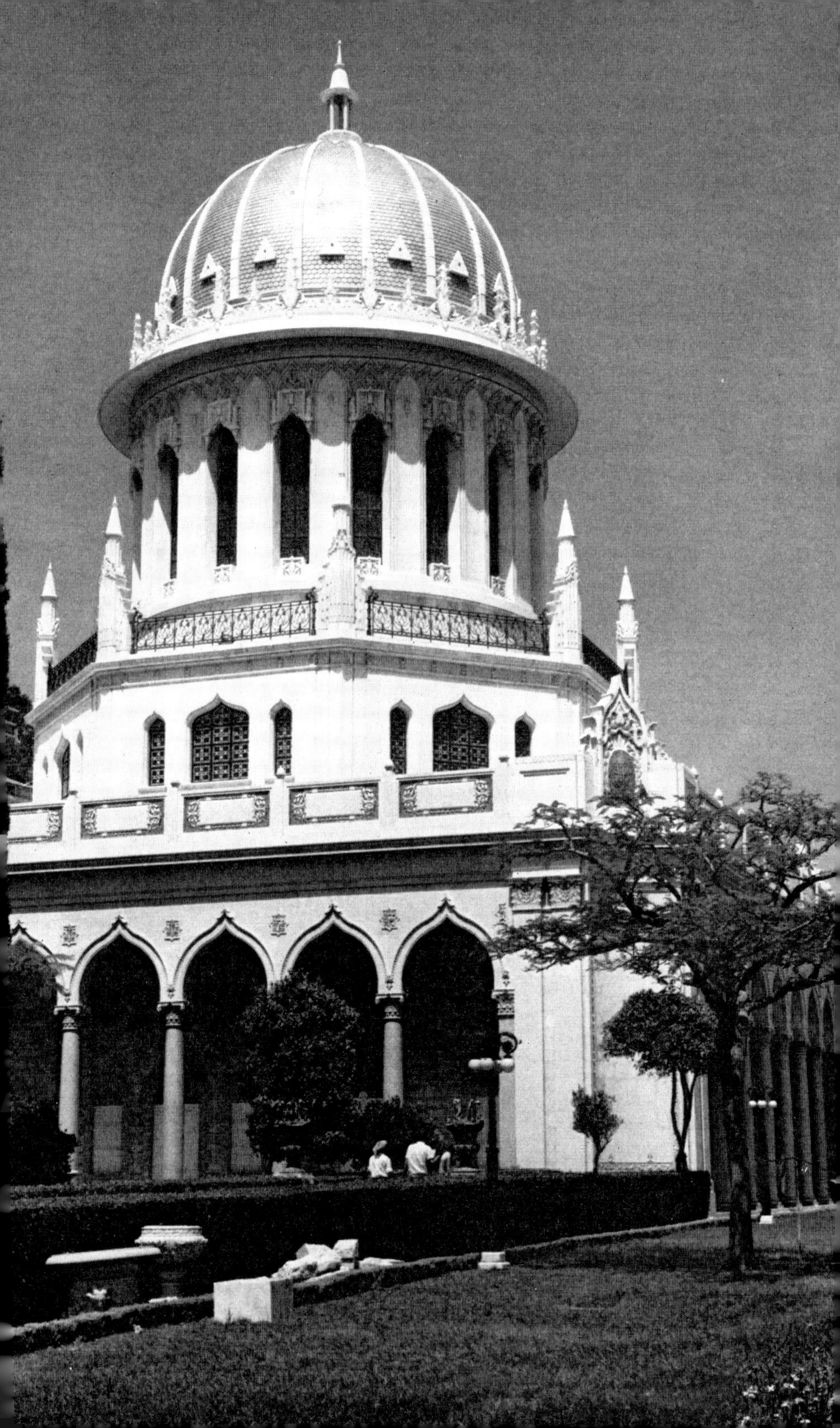

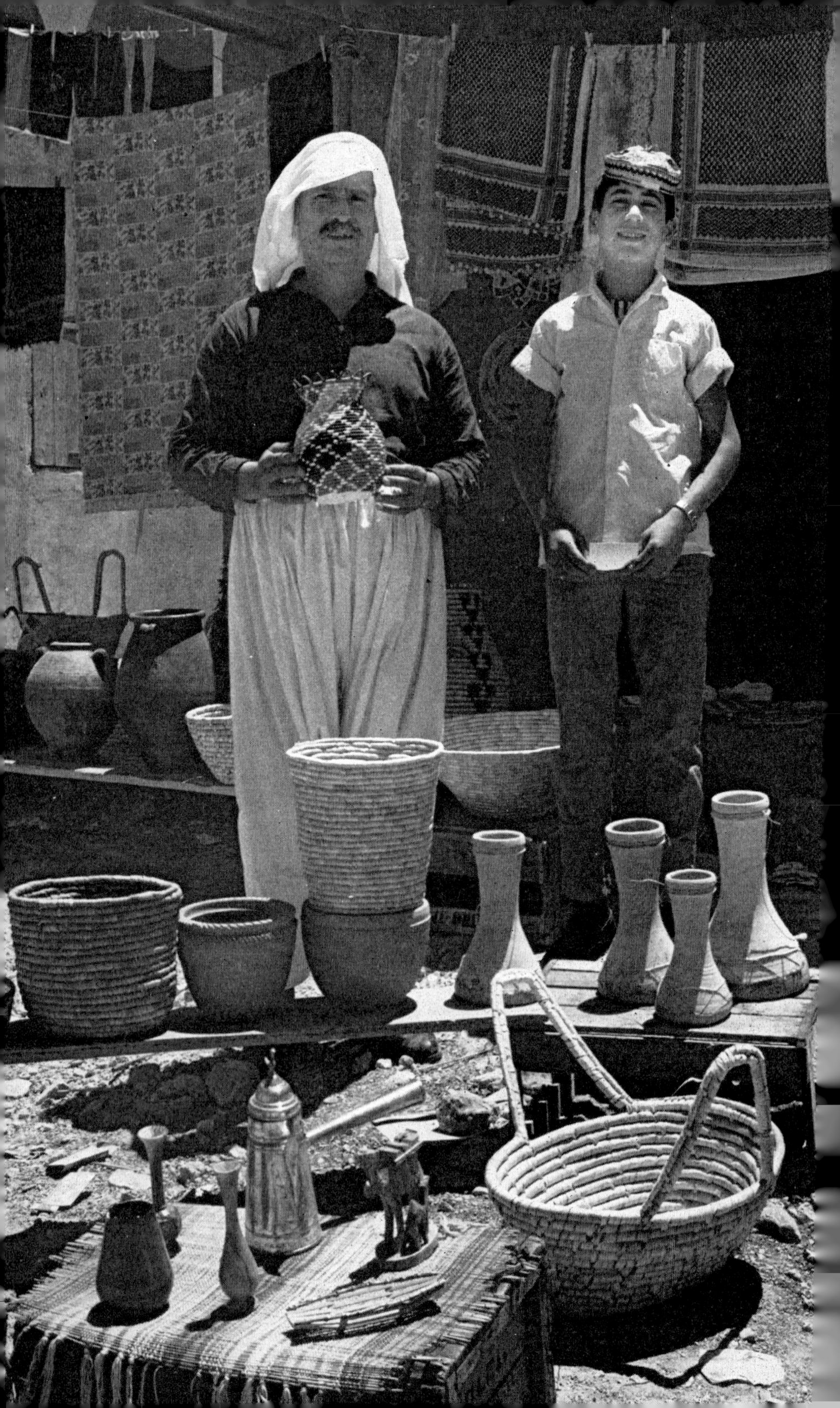

are, nominally at least, segregated in prayer by a low fence. To visit the Wall, even to those rather less than devout, is a moving experience. Almost legendary in its history, it is after all the most sacred Jewish site in the world and its restoration a matter of awe felt almost beyond words. It is a sign of devotion to kiss the stones and in the evening, when beads of dew appear on them, it is said that they weep for the fall of the Temple.

On the High Holy Days of the New Year, people mass from all over the country and, indeed, the world to celebrate the Festivals; to mourn the destruction of the Temple and observe the Day of Atonement; to dance at the Rejoicing of the Law. They come too on the three great Pilgrim Festivals—Passover, Succot and Shevuot. The last is a June festival and, a few days beforehand in 1967, an Israeli commander drove into Old Jerusalem under the heraldic lions of St Stephen's Gate to the Wall and the Temple Mount. Battle-toughened young sabras wept as they kissed the Wall and prayed—using cartridge belts as prayer-shawls. The following week, 250,000 Jews celebrated Shevuot there, the greatest gathering since Roman times, when the Temple still stood.

The dead too are honoured, out on the far western edge of the city where the unbearably poignant memorial of Yad Vashem stands on Har Hazikaron, the Hill of Remembrance. An eternal flame burns in memory of the six million Jewish victims of the Nazis. The tree-planted Avenue of the Just commemorates, with each tree, a non-Jew's courage in helping a Jew, recalling the Hasidic legend that the world is redeemed in each generation by 12 'Just Men', righteous and unknown. In the military cemetery nearby are the graves of the more recent dead, killed in the battles for Jerusalem; further again, the tomb of Theodor Herzl, founder and visionary of Zionism, its steps traced in the archives and library of the Museum here.

8 Druse shopkeeper and son in a village near Haifa

E

The namesake of Herzl's dream stands to the south of the Old City—the Zion that gave its name to Jerusalem. The road climbs Mount Zion gently, overlooked by the towers and conical roof of the Dormition Abbey on land that was the Sultan's gift to the Kaiser. Christians make their way here to visit the Cenacle, Room of the Last Supper, a vaulted Crusader hall on the traditional site. Here too in the maze of medieval buildings stands the Tomb of David, king of Israel, a dim red-draped sarcophagus gleaming faintly with candles and the silver ornaments of Torah scrolls. A yeshivah, or Jewish seminary, lodges here unofficially known as the 'hippy' yeshiva because its students may be converts to Judaism and dress informally; and because girls are also permitted to study, in segregation, a less advanced course. In such an atmosphere, it is an enlightening if strange experience to see a Japanese convert in the tiny snack-bar, wearing anorak, jeans and orthodox skullcap. Behind the yeshivah in the unobtrusive Chamber of the Martyrs lodge Jewish ritual objects salvaged from Nazi Europe.

David built his city to the east of Mount Zion, on the ridge of Ophel between Kidron and the Valley of the Cheesemakers. It lay north to south, a long narrow strip outside the present location of the city walls (which changed many times over the centuries). He bought the Jebusite's threshing-floor on which to build the Temple and, when he died, was buried in the royal city—the privilege of kings. The Pool of Siloam stands at the southern boundary, fed by its source at the Gihon fountain. The water flows through nearly 2000 feet of tunnel, cut into the solid rock by King Hezekiah to help the city withstand the siege of the Assyrians. The tunnelling teams of men began at each end and met in the middle, so finely engineered was the project—and it is possible to walk through the tunnel even today.

But whatever great feats were performed by others—Solomon after all built the Temple and the engineering of Hezekiah was a tremendous achievement—it is the spirit of David that lingers here and claims the city. His tomb is a place of prayer and lit candles, as that of a saint; and also a place for celebration and the traditional festivities of Barmitzvah (confirmation) and wedding.

On one memorable evening, the wedding that took place was between an orthodox girl and a Negro convert, a student at the yeshiva. Guests gathered in a low vaulted hall adjoining the Tomb and followed the bride to the sunken courtyard where the wedding would take place, according to orthodox tradition, in the open air. Around the courtyard, on steps and low walls, they witnessed the ceremony being held craning for a glimpse of the bride and groom who were almost hidden by the wedding canopy and the four enormous students who held it. Evening fell and the courtyard lightened with torches; a grace was said and the feast began, amid the songs; the men danced in a great circle—rabbis, massive as patriarchs, little boys in wellingtons, their sidelocks flying, shirt-sleeved students—leaping like David before the Ark. The women danced more gently around the bride. Faces flushed with heat and wine and movement. Someone fainted, someone else (a slim yeshivah youth) did a balancing trick with beer bottles. Then a hiatus to restore decorum while students and rabbis in turn fervently called down the Seven Blessings upon the bride and groom. It was far into the night and outside, the hills of Judea were dark and quiet; and the guests paused for a moment under the cold Jerusalem stars before starting down the sides of Mount Zion towards home.

4. Acre to Ashkelon

Much of Israel's history is written on its coastline. Its oldest city, Jaffa, rivals Jerusalem in age; the very name of Caesarea records the Roman Conquest; Acre and Ashkelon were built in Biblical times and figure largely in the events of that period. But the coastline also links some of the most modern towns in the country, often built near or around the sites of their historical counterparts, maintaining or reviving a continuity that, in some cases, extends over thousands of years.

The scenery is sufficiently enticing in itself to make the trip a pleasure—the beaches, the sea glittering in the distance, the orange groves and fields of the kibbutzim of the Sharon Plain. The distances are comparitively short so the visitor has time to take in his impressions, to enquire and delve into the past, never far from the reassuring amenities of the present; or, indeed, from the ambitious goals of the future.

Acre is not only one of the world's oldest cities, it is also one of the most strategically placed and, therefore, coveted by all the nations anxious to secure a hold on the area to the north. It has been besieged on innumerable occasions from Biblical to modern times, repulsing many would-be invaders and falling to others. Situated on the coastal plain in a natural harbour, Acre lay on the route to Phoenicia and dominated the threshold to the North, sometimes described as the Gateway to Galilee. This fact alone explains why the ground around the city was so often trampled by so many invading armies—its strategic situation, straddling a small peninsula between Mount Carmel and Tyre, was never underestimated.

Joshua attempted unsuccessfully to dislodge the Canaanites in his day and Simon the Maccabee also failed to take the city. The Crusaders were more successful—during the First Crusade, they captured first Jerusalem and then Acre, renaming it St John of Acre after their patron saint. In 1187, Saladin the Saracen took the city from them but it was recaptured by Richard the Lionheart shortly after. When the Crusaders lost Jerusalem, Acre became the capital from which they governed and the city's fall in 1291 ended the dominance of the Crusaders in the Holy Land.

In the eighteenth century, it was once again an important prize. Napoleon besieged the city in 1799 but failed to take it. This defeat was the reason that he finally gave up his Near East campaign. Napoleon's difficulties were caused by the destruction of his fleet at the Battle of the Nile and the capture of his siege guns by the British on their way to Acre.

The final episode in its military history occurred when the Israelis, in their War of Independence, took Acre in 1949—by a brilliant naval operation, as the first Crusaders had done centuries earlier.

The city affords the visitor an attractive view of minarets, domes and palm trees against the sea and sky. The old walled centre of Acre has a distinct flavour of its own, dominated by the Turkish period architecture. The other parts of Acre are new suburbs, built by the Israelis during the last decade. But the characteristic feature of the town remains Turkish, due to the efforts of the Ottoman Governor who repulsed Napoleon's attack, Ahmed Jezzar Pasha (Ahmed the Butcher). His ambition was to create a 'little Constantinople' at the turn of the eighteenth century—and he almost succeeded. Courtyards and fountains, the marble columns of old mosques, combine to give this city its pronounced profile. Old Acre is a maze of lanes and winding alleys, housing mixed communities of Arabs, and Christians, and

Jewish immigrants from the four corners of the earth. The Turkish Bathhouse, now a museum, is one of the many structures that, like the magnificent city wall, remind one of the city's splendid past. The bazaar, with its bustle and colourful wares, is a tourist meeting-place, offering the sight of donkeys carrying a variety of goods from traditional Arab pottery to vegetables from the Galilee; and the sounds of many languages and the excitement of the traditional market place reflect the daily life of a busy oriental town.

The Crypt of St John is situated nearby and the entrance can be reached directly from the bazaar. The vaulted hall was uncovered by excavation and it is thought to have belonged to the Order of St John used by the Hospitallers as their refectory. There is a secret tunnel leading to the sea which must have given them direct access to their ships. Other tunnels thread the city beneath the streets, further proof perhaps that it once belonged to the Crusaders. Beneath this, a Roman city existed, judging by remains already uncovered.

Acre reached its heyday as a commercial centre under the Crusaders and merchants from many parts of the country were attracted by its amenities. It has always harboured Jews and, during Turkish times, many Kabbalists (followers of the esoteric sect of Judaism) settled in the port. The British captured it but preferred living in Haifa and Acre gradually declined into little more than a large fishing village.

In Ottoman times, and during the British mandate, prisoners were confined in Acre jail, which stood on the foundation of a Crusader structure. The Citadel, as it was called, was the scene of a famous jail-break of Jewish guerillas in 1947. They were resistance fighters of the underground movement of the time, and the tablets in the former execution chamber—which has been transformed into a small museum—record the names of the men who were hanged. (Another important prisoner once held in the jail was Baha-Ulla, the founder of the Bahai sect. He spent 24 years within its walls before his release in 1892, and he is buried a mile to the north of Acre where his house and tomb have become important relics).

Another landmark of the city is the 'Turkish Tower', at the entrance to the Khan el-Umdan. The Khan—its name translates as hostelry, or caravanserai—has a fine atmosphere of the past, with its great courtyard and numerous porches built over the remains of a Dominican monastery. There are two other hostelries in Acre, the Khan el-Afranj and the Khan el-Shawarda, both built over Christian foundations.

The highway south leads from Turkish past to Israeli present. Along the road, as it travels the eight miles to Haifa, are industrial plants and refineries and modern low-cost housing. Haifa is Israel's largest port, a modern city with not much trace of the Orient about it. In contrast to Acre, a city full of the splendour of its Turkish and Crusader past, Haifa is matter-of-fact and orderly. Nevertheless, it is one of the most beautiful ports in the world. The sweep of the blue bay rising to Mount Carmel is a sight no-one forgets easily, whether he travels by road or one of the many ships that call in the bustling harbour.

Haifa was bypassed in Biblical times, when other towns along the coast were more easily accessible by road. Nevertheless, excavations show that settlements always existed here. Historically, there are associations with the prophet Elijah, who was thought to have once sought refuge in a cave below a promontory of Mount Carmel. It was understandable, therefore, that the Carmelites, who adopted Elijah as their patron saint, chose Haifa as the site for their monastery in the thirteenth century. Pilgrims still seek out this holy place of prayer, situated above the cave and known as the School of Prophets. In the 1860s, a German colony was established here by the Templars. Their descendants were treated as enemy aliens during the First World War and many emigrated, but the buildings survive as part of the attractions of the city.

Theodor Herzl, founder father of Zionism, was enchanted with Haifa and envisaged its development from the sleepy fishing village it then was to a prosperous metropolis, humming with industry and attracting world-wide trade. In his novel *Altneuland* (Old New Land), he describes the image of this future town and it is truly amazing that, although he wrote the novel in 1902, Herzl foresaw so much of what was to be.

Israel's second largest town has no funicular railway as prophesied by Herzl but it does possess the country's only underground, which transports passengers to and from the mountain top. The port is diversified and so busy that another deepwater harbour had to be built at Ashdod to take the pressure off Haifa. The city, spreading out from the harbour, has an oil refinery and numerous industries ranging from desalination and plastics to textiles, chemicals, soap and wine.

Haifa has been described as a cake with several layers. The lowest layer is the port with its industrial belt, the commercial layer is above it and the topmost layer is residential. The open-air cafés have a Central European touch and the parks and gardens that are very much a characteristic of the city show its residents' determination to create a town that is habitable and can control the inevitable influences that threaten every major port. The progressive spirit displayed proves that co-operation between Arab and Jewish city councillors is not merely a dream of the future. The emphasis on civic activities and amenities for the young is strong, while Haifa's museums display the treasures of archaeology and modern art that this old/new city has to offer.

The highest layer is, of course, Mount Carmel. It has become the residential area that Herzl hoped for and, with its pine forests and splendid views over the bay and the Galilee mountains, one of the most sought-after. The houses range from modest bungalows to millionaires' villas. There are a number of hotels and, as on the lower layers, street cafés are popular. An open-air stadium is in full use and the fortunate students of the Haifa Technion have their campus here, in one of the country's finest universities.

The loveliest building in Haifa is the Bahai Shrine, gleaming and serene on the Carmel slopes. The Bahai sect is of Persian origin, believing in the One God and attempting to draw on the teachings of Judaism, Christianity and Islam for the spiritual solutions to the problems of the world. It has many followers throughout the world who come to Haifa as pilgrims. The majority of visitors, however, come rather for the beauty of its architecture and, in particular, the terraced Persian garden, splendidly lined with towering cypresses. Above them, the shrine's golden dome rises against the hillside.

Haifa's development stems from the British occupation. During the mandate, Haifa Bay was used extensively for shipping and this period saw the building of the modern port, as well as an oil pipeline to Iraq. With Independence came a change in Haifa's fortunes. Trade with the Arab countries was dislocated and the oil pipeline cut, along with the railway link. Nevertheless, the port recovered and has since flourished. The oil refinery is now in full swing and a new pipeline connects it to Eilat. Memories of the ships laden with refugees, whose anguish marked the period of British mandate, have been expunged by other shipping, by modern cargo boats and by Israel's own Merchant Navy based in Haifa Bay.

The Fleet is younger than the country's independence. Arab boycott has made expansion a major necessity. The Merchant Marine that numbered only 30 ships in the mid-50s had expanded to 120 vessels by 1972 with a total tonnage of about 3.3 millions. Israeli manpower is in short supply and efforts are being made to train more Israelis to man the ships. The servicing of this new fleet alone, is a major job for Haifa, a task it shares with Ashdod. The port's possession was fiercely debated prior to Independence. During the mandate period, relationships between Arab and Jew were good. Jewish and Arab representatives sat together on civil committees. But this changed overnight. Shortly before the May Independence of 1948 Haganah troops occupied strategic points in the port and the Arabic quarter. As elsewhere, the Arabs moved out despite offers of full protection and Haifa became a Jewish port.

The Carmel range which dominates Haifa has been the home

of man from the Stone-Age through Biblical times to the present day. Several Druze villages nestle in the mountains and their inhabitants are regular and colourful visitors to the city, adding to its cosmopolitan atmosphere. More elegantly, the artist's colony of Ein Hod rests at the foothills, in what was once an Arab village. Even now, its most sophisticated building is the pleasantly set-out gallery displaying for sale a variety of prints, sculpture, local pottery, ceramics and jewellery. It is an attractively artificial enclave of immense charm and exotic inhabitants.

Another lovely village in the foothills is Zichron Ya'akov, renowned for its wine. It owes its existence to Baron Edmond de Rothschild who founded it in 1882. Zichron Ya'akov is proud of its high quality grapes and is a major attraction during the autumn, when Israelis come to celebrate the grape harvest. Both Baron de Rothschild and his wife are buried here.

Between Ein Hod and Zichron Ya'akov is a Crusader ruin, the Castle Athlit. It dates back to the twelfth century as a Templar stronghold, one of the network of castles which had been established throughout the Holy Land. Athlit was of importance to the Crusaders during the period following Saladin's capture of Jerusalem. It is situated on a promonotory across a moat which the Templars had built, and comprises a massive series of walls and turrets. Today Athlit is also part of Israel's defences and off limits to visitors.

South of Athlit lies Caesarea. It is reached by a short turn-off three miles north of Hadera on the main Tel Aviv Haifa road. A description of this 'gracious vacation spot', with the blue waters of the Mediterranean rolling gently upon 'the most beautiful beach in all Israel' was as true in the times of the Romans, 2000 years ago, as it is now. This pearl on the coastal strip was ignored for a long time, buried under the sand dunes until the archaeologists turned their attention to it. Today, Caesarea's past is as much of an attraction as its present—a brash modern seaside resort with discothèques, water sports and magnificent holiday villas.

This fascinating town was originally named as a token of

Herod's gratitude to his Roman masters who placed him on the throne of Judea. The chosen site was a Phoenician anchorage called Strato's Tower and the work, begun in 22 BC, took 12 years to complete and to satisfy Herod's grandiose ideas. Flavius Josephus, the historian, had this to say of his impression:

> When he observed that there was a city by the seaside that was much decayed, but that the place, by the happiness of its situation, was capable of great improvements, he rebuilt it all with white stone, and adorned with several most splendid places ... for the case was this, that all the sea-shore between Dora and Joppa, in the middle of which this city is situated had no good haven, in so much as everyone that sailed from Phoenicia for Egypt was obliged to lie in the stormy sea. ... But the King overcame nature, and built a haven larger than was Piraus (near Athens) with a quay which ran round the entire haven.

The deep-sea harbour that turned Caesarea into a maritime city was a tremendously advanced engineering operation. The town itself, judging by the reports of Josephus, must have been magnificent. Remarking on the white houses, he described how they adjoined the harbour, the streets converging on the sea; and talked of 'Caesar's Temple', remarkable for its beauty and fine proportions. Herod also constructed an amphitheatre and marketplace and built the hippodrome outside the city walls, for the games he appointed to take place every fifth year.

Caesarea was so highly thought of, that it became the seat of the Roman procurators in Judea some 10 years after Herod's death. One of the most important archaeological finds was that of a stone with the name 'Pontius Pilate' engraved on it. The name until then had only been recorded in the Gospels and the works of Josephus. It was in Caesarea that the Jews began their revolt in AD 66, when the Roman general Vespasian was quartered in the town. The Jews fought both the Romans and the Syrians, (the episode having been sparked off by a dispute with the Syrians), and 20,000 were massacred. This in turn set off the Great Jewish War, which was to end in the destruction of the Second Temple. Four years later, after the fall of Jerusalem and the destruction of the Second Temple in AD 70, Titus came to Caesarea to celebrate his victory with a series of games, in the course of which 2,500 Jewish prisoners were killed. On the same spot, a happier festival took place in 1961, when a historic concert was held on the site of the excavated Roman theatre, during which performances were given by such performers as Pablo Casals, Rudolf Serkin, Isaac Stern, Leonard Rose, Eugene Istomin and the Budapest Quartet.

During the second and third centuries the Jews returned and founded schools and synagogues; and eminent scholars established their homes in the city. Caesarea also became the centre of the new religion, Christianity, and it is often named in the Acts of the Apostles. St Peter baptized his first Gentile converts there, and the Roman centurion Cornelius and his family. St Paul was brought to the city as a prisoner where he demanded to be judged by Caesar and King Agrippa sent him to Rome (Acts 25–26).

Roman rule ended in AD 639 with the Arab invasion. Caesarea was the last Byzantine city in Palestine to surrender, and did so after a lengthy siege. The Crusaders took the city in 1101, but its old glory was not revived, the Crusaders confining themselves to a narrow area, concentrating their main forces at Acre. During fierce battles over the following 40 years, Caesarea changed hands several times. In 1251, towards the end of the Crusader period, Louis IX of France built the city's fortifications, the remains of which can still be seen. The last battle took place in 1265, when Crusader defences crumbled and much of Caesarea was destroyed.

With the return of the Jews to Palestine, kibbutz Sdot Yam, a fishing co-operative, was set up in 1937, near the perimeter of the Roman city. In 1959, the Caesarea Development Corporation was established jointly by the government and Baron Edmond de

Rothschild. The Corporation was given land by the government and Rothschild holdings, acquired 80 years previously.

The Rothschild family also constructed Israel's only 18-hole golf course, one of the main sporting attractions of the new garden city. The sportsmen who swing their golf clubs against the background of Roman arches, the riders who pound along the beach near a second-century aqueduct, the divers near Herod's submerged harbour, all might be too preoccupied with the present to think about the past. That job they can safely leave to the archaeologists and historians for whom Caesarea is one vast 'dig'. An Italian expedition unearthed the Roman theatre in 1961. Constructed on a cliff to the south and now restored, it is the site of the annual festival, a tradition inaugurated by the famous concert of 1961. An American expedition explored the submerged harbour, and the Government has excavated almost the whole of the moat and the Crusader city. The work of clearance and restoration is still continuing.

The reconstruction gives an excellent idea of the architecture of the city in Herod's day. The Roman Hippodrome was spacious enough to seat 20,000 spectators. A near-by road leads to the top of a mound, where a beautiful Byzantine church floor, dating back to the fifth and sixth century was discovered in 1957. Another fork on the same road shows the way to the arches of the Roman Aqueduct, recently stripped from the sand which had covered the remains of the structure that supplied the town with water from the mountains in the north.

In 1956, a Hebrew University expedition discovered the ruins of the fourth and seventh century synagogues. Further work on these sites brought other treasures to view. Byzantine remains were found just beyond the hippodrome, dating back to the fifth and sixth centuries; two massive statues, the main features of this site, are dated as early as the second and third centuries AD. The road turns from this point towards the gate of the Crusader city where the Christian conquerors built their harbour on top of the Byzantine and Roman ports.

Indeed, each period used the remains of structures of earlier times for their own building. The Byzantines used Roman statues to decorate their homes, Arabs used marble walls from Roman villas, the Crusaders used materials brought in during earlier centuries from Italy and Greece to strengthen their own fortifications. An excavated Crusader street is paved with large blocks of Roman marble. A hill which houses relics, probably of Herod's Temple, displays on its summit two Crusader buildings, one an unfinished cathedral.

A resort of quite different type is nearby Nathanya. It lies on the shore within the lovely Sharon Valley, half way between Tel Aviv and Haifa. The breath of antiquity which blows through Caesarea is absent from the orderly parks and gardens. Nathanya has its own character, an elegance and sophistication which appeals to those who like to combine their seaside pleasures with the amenties of the city. It has all the sportsman desires: perfect beaches and bathing, boats, riding, fishing and waterski-ing and excellent hotels. The town is built on twin ridges some hundred feet above sea-level. The hotels compete not only with each other in comfort, but also with entertainment provided elsewhere—the cliff-side amphitheatre concerts, nightclubs and open-air cafés.

Built in 1928, Nathanya has become the centre for one of the country's most important industries. Diamond cutting and polishing is a major export industry, an important source of income for an economy heavily dependent on foreign currency. The industry was established and developed during the Second World War, by Belgian refugees. When the war closed Antwerp to the diamond industry, the Jewish refugees took their expertise to Israel and many settled in Nathanya. Other markets developed again after the war but Nathanya had become firmly established and has now won a world-wide reputation for itself. In the wake of the diamond industry, other enterprises have also developed in this seaside town.

A few kilometers further south lies Herzlia. The modern town was named after Herzl but its ancient site has a stormy history.

There was a city here in Biblical times, built by the Canaanites. When the Greeks came to the shores of Palestine, they used the town as a port and named it Apollonia. Richard the Lionheart defended it against Saladin but the town was captured in the thirteenth century and sacked. Under Turkish rule, like other towns along the coast, it fell into neglect but with the return of the Jews in the present century, Herzlia was reborn and renamed. Over the decades, Herzlia developed into one of Israel's most attractive towns and is still expanding fast. Between the highway and the shore, the affluent villas overlook the sea and several consulates have their pleasant headquarters here.

From Tel Aviv, the coast reaches to Ashdod Yam, the new deep-sea port. The road along the way passes a number of smaller towns and villages, most notably Rishon le-Zion, Rehovot and the ancient Yavne. Rishon le-Zion, renowned for its wine industry, was founded by Russian Jewish immigrants in 1882. Without the help of Baron de Rothschild, who directed the beginnings of the viniculture and raised the necessary funds, the settlement might not have survived, in view of the problems of irrigation and climate. But, like so many other agricultural 'miracles' in the Land, it was a rewarding struggle. The fine cellars that Rothschild helped to build are still in use and wine from Rishon is exported all over the world, finding its way into Jewish homes particularly for the festive season of the New Year.

Rehovot was founded some eight years after Rishon le-Zion. It was the dream of the Zionist leader and Israel's first president, Chaim Weizmann, to live and work in Rehovot. An outstanding scientist, Dr Weizmann had a vision of a community of scientists working in the near-ideal conditions of a special research institute to be founded here. It was a bold idea, thought by some to be a visionary's dream—but the dream was fulfilled and Weizmann made his home and continued his scientific work in the town that was to become the site of the country's foremost research centre (and one of international reputation)—the Weizmann Institute.

To the south west of Rehovot lies a small village that occupies a special place in Jewry's memory—Yavneh. The story goes back some 1900 years when, according to tradition, the great Rabbi Yochanan ben Zakkai was given a special audience by the Roman authorities before the destruction of the Temple in 70 BC. He was invited to see the commander of Jerusalem and was told that he would be allowed one favour. Anxious to preserve learning and study for future generations, he asked for a safe place where he and his pupils could follow peacefully their studies of the Holy Scriptures. His request sounded simple enough, 'Give me Yavneh and seven sages' and the Romans granted his request. A famous school developed from these beginnings. Jewish learning and education received inspiration and support from the little centre at Yavneh and it was here that the Old Testament was canonized and the great work of the Mishna, the codification of Jewish law, begun. Throughout the ages, the tradition of study remained alive in the area and, today, orthodox Jewish farmers are attracted to it for this reason.

A little further south, twentieth-century Israel emerges again at Nebi Rubin. An atomic reactor squats among the sand dunes here, its radioactive isotopes used for medical and agricultural research. This is not the only nuclear reactor in the country—there is one near Arad, in the Negev—but it does symbolize the great technological achievements that, among other things, may one day solve completely the problem of desalination of sea water for irrigation purposes.

Fifteen miles along the coast, the port of Ashdod Yam overlooks the bleak sand dunes. It was established five kilometers north of the ancient Biblical city of the Philistines, that perennial thorn in Israel's side at the time of Judges before King David put an end to the menace. It was to Ashdod that the Philistines brought the Ark when they captured it, placing it in the temple of Dazgon their god. The first Book of Samuel recounts that the statue of

9   *Roman ruins in Caesarea*

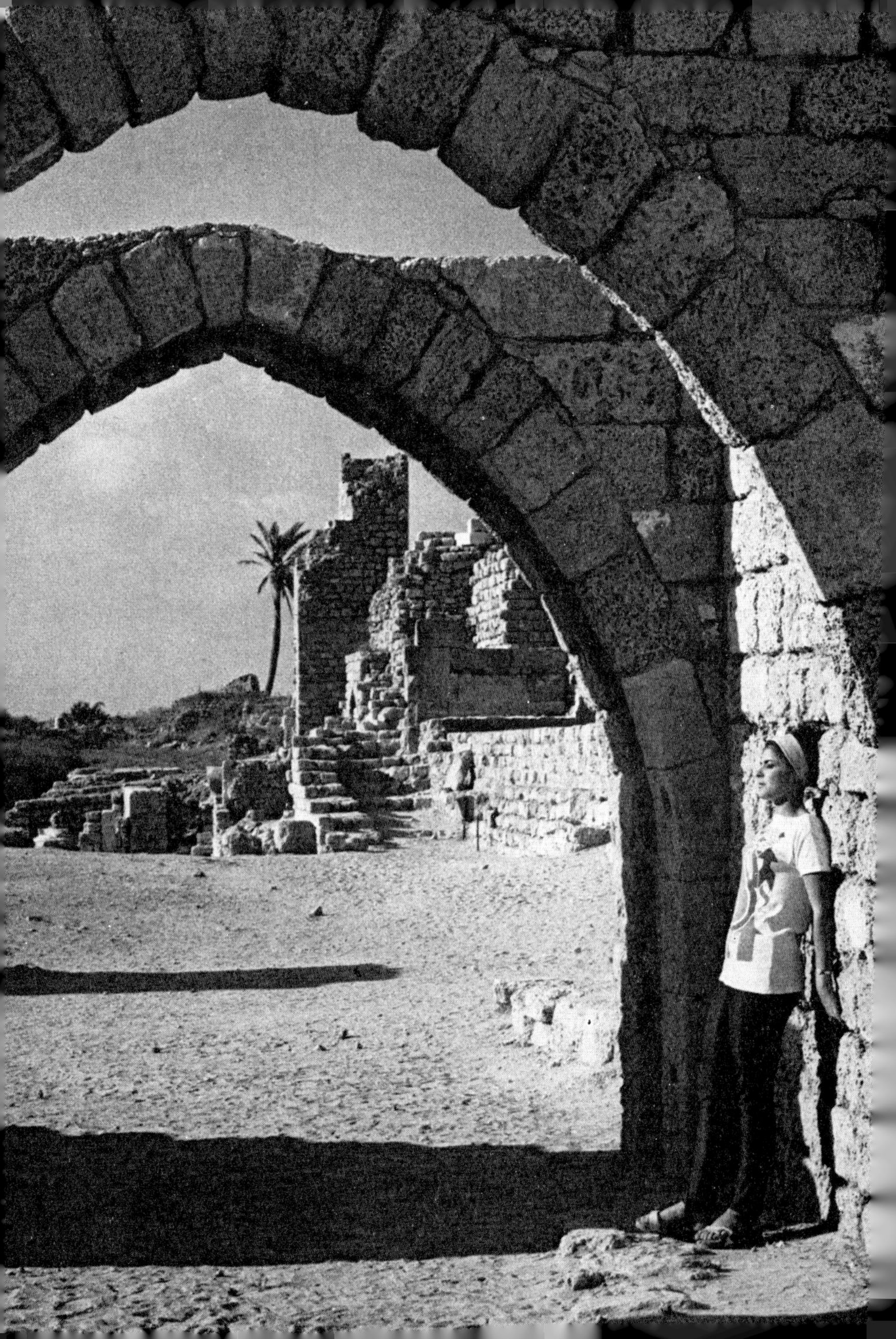

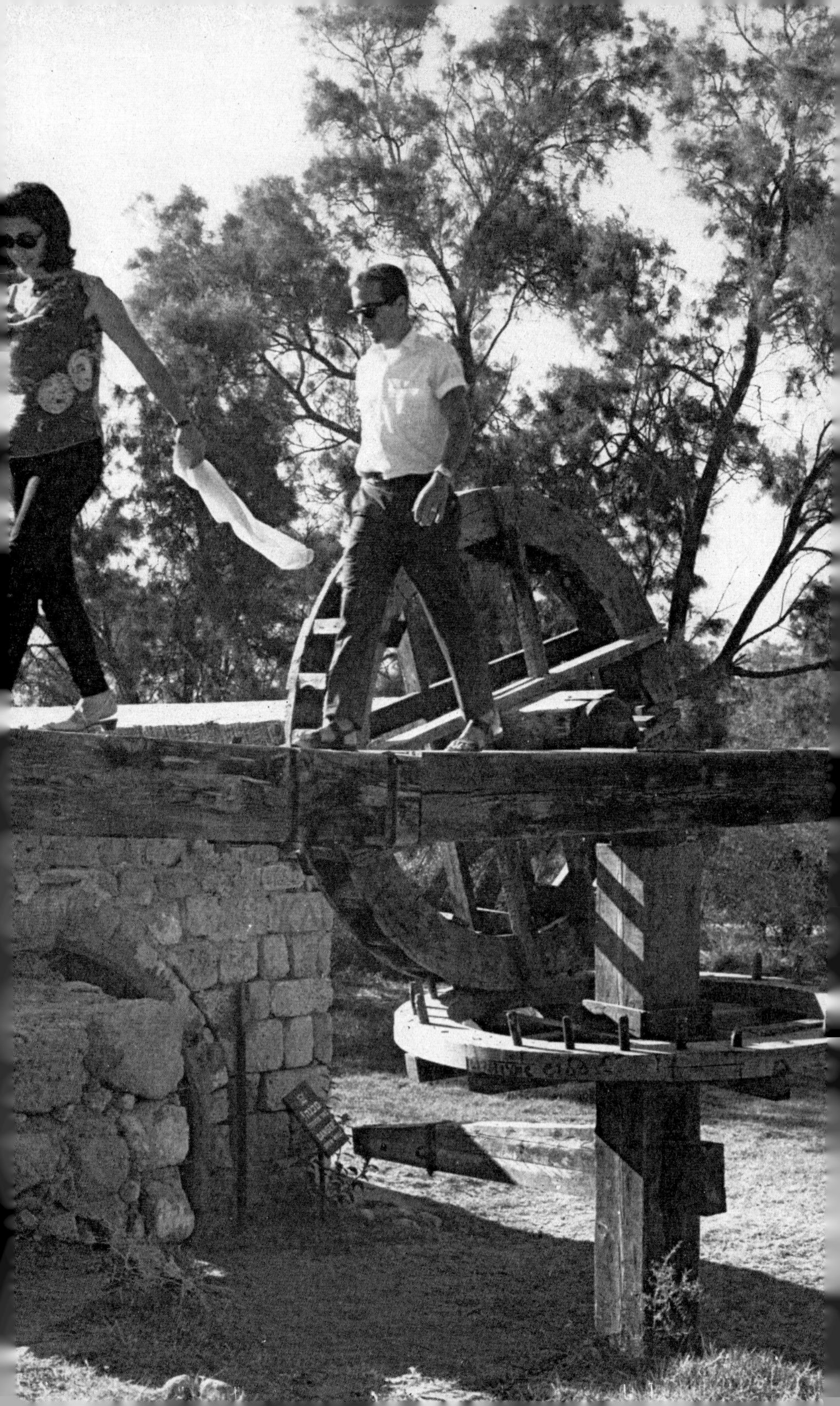

Dagon was found fallen before the Ark the next day, and that the Ashdodites were smitten with a deadly disease. The Philistines, fearing they would suffer the same fate as the Egyptians before the Exodus, returned the Ark seven months later (with 'trespass offerings' for compensation) to the Israelites. Mentioned a number of times in the Bible, all that remains of the city is its tel, or mound, which can still be seen.

The modern port was created by the necessity to divert traffic from Haifa, whose capacity was certain to be over-extended as the country expanded rapidly. Patient research established the best area for a new deep-sea harbour and, after feasibility studies of sea and winds, Ashdod was chosen as the site. It was not a natural harbour and every inch of the port had to be physically constructed. Today, citrus fruits and minerals such as potash and phosphates are mechanically loaded direct from shore to ship. Even by Israeli standards, Ashdod Yam is a fast-growing city. Its blueprint visualized a population of 250,000 in a pleasant garden milieu and, judging by the avenues of shade-giving date palms now firmly rooted in the sandy soil after being brought here by the truckload, the town is off to a promising start. A naval training centre has been established here, industrial plants have been set up around the harbour area and a crude oil pipeline built to connect it with Eilat.

Its nearest neighbour, Ashkelon, lies some five miles south along the coast. In many ways, it is a counterpart to the city at the beginning of this journey down Israel's shoreline, Acre. Both trace their origins back to an ancient past, both have had a rich and unsettled history, both have known the stamp of successive civilizations and both have great scenic beauty.

Ancient Ashkelon was an important harbour situated at the mouth of a river long since silted up. Good soil and ample water supplies drew men to the area throughout the ages and within an

10 *Ashkelon: ancient water wheel in the ruins of Herod's palace*

archaeological tel, six different levels of early settlement have been uncovered—Canaanite, Philistine, Greco-Roman, Byzantine, Muslim, Crusader—each one built on the site of its predecessor. The modern Ashkelon is a popular seaside resort (with the irresistibly-named Antiquities' Beach and Samson's Beach) with a wealth of sporting facilities. It is also a market town—new Ashkelon, like the old, is a farming centre—and a number of flourishing light industries have made their home here.

In Biblical times, Ashkelon was associated with the Philistines, the people who, when attempting to settle in Canaan, frequently clashed with the Israelites. The countryside around Ashkelon was the scene of the heroic deeds of young Samson of whom the Bible recounts: 'the Spirit of the Lord came upon him and he went down to Ashkelon and slew thirty men of them and took their spoil . . .' XIV, I9) Samson, after having been betrayed and taken prisoner, killed 3,000 of their men in Gaza, another Philistinian settlement not far from Ashkelon, by using his supernatural strength to bring down the temple pillars, crushing himself and all within those walls.

In his lament over the death of King Saul and his son Jonathan David cried out: 'Tell it not in Gath, publish it not in the streets of Ashkelon; lest the daughters of the Philistines rejoice, lest the daughters of the uncircumcised triumph'. (Samuel I, 20) Still it is unlikely that the streets of Ashkelon did not resound, even in those days of poor communications, at the news of the end of Saul's dynasty.

The Hebrew prophets ranted against Ashkelon, with Amos prophecying death to 'him that holdeth the sceptre of Ashkelon' (Amos I, 8) and Zephania forecasting the fall of the city. 'And the coast shall be for the remnant of the house of Judah . . . in the houses of Ashkelon shall they lie down in the evening . . .' (Zephania II, 7) Is it perhaps lack of diplomacy that the main street of modern Ashkelon is called Zephania Boulevard?

The Assyrians, Babylonians and Persians have all left their mark on the town. Ashkelon was an important centre in Hellenistic times and Greek sculptures are among those recovered from excavations. Josephus described Herod's interest in the town to which he added considerable architectural adornments. Jews were a minority after Ashkelon became a Christian city in Byzantine times. The Crusaders conquered it in 1153 and its masters changed a number of times before it was finally destroyed by the Sultan Baybars in 1270. The Ottomans built a fort on its site but the actual restoration of the town came with the independence of Israel in 1948.

To the south of the city a national park has been created to preserve and exhibit the archaeological discoveries. Major excavations had been carried out in the early twenties by a British team, which first located the 'tel'—the site of ancient Ashkelon which now forms the southern side of the park. The mound slopes down to the beach where the ruins of an ancient sea wall mark the old city's boundaries. Roman columns are a feature of the wall which, itself, is of the later Byzantine era.

The visitor to the tel can view innumerable relics, from the famous statue of the goddess of victory with the globe of the world resting on Atlas' shoulder, to tablets from ancient synagogues. The main archaeological attraction is the group of Greek and Roman sculptures.

Above the park the ruins of the wall is a remnant of the Crusader period and about a mile away, not far from the busy beach is a Roman tomb, dating back to the third century.

Despite its venerable past, modern Ashkelon is a very young town indeed. It was founded with Israel's independence and, of its five districts, one was established as recently as 1952 by South African Jewry. Ashkelon was granted the status of a city in 1955 and has thrived ever since. Its popularity is partly due to the near-ideal climate it enjoys, with cool sea-breezes tempering the dry desert temperatures of the Negev.

5. Judea and Samaria

Judea and Samaria are, in a sense, the waistline of Israel, sprawling between Galilee and the Negev. A somewhat more defined description would call it the West Bank, although its Biblical appellations are in common use. It was a part of mandate Palestine before it was taken by the Arab forces (mainly Jordanian) following the 1948 war, which pared the land between Haifa and Tel Aviv into a narrow strip (in some places, as little as 10 miles wide). Under Israeli administration since 1967, the ceasefire line now bisects the Jordan Valley down the centre. The area is predominantly Muslim (there are a small number of Christians dwelling mainly in Bethlehem and Ramallah), roughly a quarter of whom live in refugee camps. While the situation is not ideal, it should be noted that by Israel's 'open bridges' policy West Bank Arabs can travel freely between Israel and Arab countries, can obtain permission for relatives to visit from Arab states (over 100,000 in 1971), hold their own municipal elections and participate in health, welfare and social services of the country; while the camps themselves are getting a facelift and the inhabitants are free to work in the West Bank or in Israel.

From a different point of view, the area is a significant part of the Holy Land and a great deal of Biblical history was enacted here. The town called Samaria was, in fact, the capital of the ancient kingdom of northern Israel, and the name Samaritan derives from here.

The major city in Judea is Jerusalem and their fortunes were often linked. Over the centuries, the kingdom shrank almost to the boundaries of its capital on more than one occasion, when conquest eroded its borders.

To the west, the Judean hills begin midway between Jerusalem and the sea. The monastery of Latrun stands here, a pleasant landmark on the main Tel Aviv-Jerusalem highway, where the monks sell some of the finest wines in Israel. In more sombre vein, Latrun Police Station was the scene of bitter fighting in 1948, when Ben Gurion, then Prime Minister, sent hundreds of newly-arrived, untrained immigrants against the Arab Legion entrenched in the police station in a desperate and tragically misguided attempt to capture the highway. North-west, the road leading to Ramallah through a picturesque rural landscape is now being widened to take pressure off the main route from Tel Aviv.

The road now starts to climb gradually to Jerusalem. The passes of Sha'ar Hagai and Bab-el-Wad are lined with burnt-out trucks in memory of the desperate Jewish attempts to run the gauntlet of the Arab-held hills to bring food and ammunition to the defenders of besieged Jerusalem. The city was in danger of falling when an archaeologist's map revealed an ancient road, long since covered over, to the south. It formed the basis of the new 'Burma Road', cleared and rebuilt by immense efforts around the clock, from Ramla to Abu Ghosh near Jerusalem. The trucks had their alternative supply route, and the city was saved.

Abu Ghosh was the only Arab village friendly to Israel at that time, sheltering and aiding Jewish fighters. The villagers trace their ancestry back to an enterprising Bedouin bandit who became prosperous by exacting considerable tolls from travellers 150 years ago. The village stands on the site of Kiryat Yearim, mentioned in Chronicles, where the Ark of the Covenant rested after it had been in the keeping of the Philistines; and from here, David brought it up to Jerusalem. 'Thus all Israel brought up the Ark of the Covenant of the Lord with shouting and with sound of the cornet . . .' and David danced before it into the city.

Jerusalem is an excellent base from which to visit the southern region of Judea. The road winds east of the city with the Mount of Olives on its right, to the fork that leads either north to Jericho or south to Bethlehem. The latter road was the ancient caravaneers' route, smoothed and widened under Jordanian administration to serve travellers from the Jordan-held eastern sector of Jerusalem, to Bethlehem and Hebron. The southern route cuts through the Kidron Valley lengthwise, hugging the picturesque matchbox village of Silwan; then twists and turns around the Mount of Scandal and the Mount of Offence (so named because Solomon worshipped idols here). In the distance, the Herodion and the Dead Sea shimmer in the haze and the leisurely journey to Bethlehem, which should take about half an hour, may take twice as long depending on the traffic, goats and sheep along the way.

A few kilometers outside Jerusalem lies Ramat Rachel. This kibbutz was established in 1925 and, like many others in Israel, has had more than its fair share of history. It was heavily fought over in 1948 and exchanged hands several times during some of the bloodiest battles of the war, until it was finally regained by the Israeli forces. It is also the site of some of the most interesting of the area's 'digs'—a cluster of impressive ruins of the palace of Jehoiachim, king of Judah in the seventh century BC, in addition to a number of Roman dwellings. The road goes even deeper into history, passing Rachel's Tomb as it approaches Bethlehem's outskirts. The Tomb is regarded as the third holiest Jewish shrine after the Western Wall and the Tomb of the Patriarchs (of which Rachel's is the only tomb outside Machpela). The building itself goes back only as far as the nineteenth century, when it was built by the Anglo-Jewish philanthropist, Sir Moses Montefiore (who also erected the famous windmill in Jerusalem), but its atmosphere is largely dissipated by its position alongside the busy road. However, the Tomb's great religious importance brings a constant flow of devout Jewish pilgrims, and Muslims—since Islam also reveres the Jewish Patriarchs—join the faithful waiting to enter the shrine where '(Rachel) died and was buried on the way to Ephrath, which is Bethlehem . . .' as recorded in the Book of Genesis.

Bethlehem is a hilly, picturesque town its skyline dominated by the crosses of its many churches, monasteries and hospices. It is mentioned many times in the Old Testament in connection with Rachel, with the story of Ruth and with her descendant, David, who was born here. And it is, of course, the site of the Nativity. Its Christian associations would be apparent (even without the crosses) from the moment of entering the town in names like Shepherd's Field, where a small chapel commemorates the place where the shepherds were told of Jesus' birth, and Manger Square, where a kind of natural division seems to take place between the Church of the Nativity at one end and shops, mosque and police station at the other.

The Church was first built by Constantine, that ubiquitous patron of religious architecture. Destroyed during the Samarian revolt 200 years later, it was rebuilt by Justinian and, later still, underwent a good deal of restoration both by the Crusaders in the eleventh and twelfth centuries, and in the mid-nineteenth century. The Crusader arch in the main gate was reduced in size to about four feet high and became known as the 'door of humility' because it was—and is—necessary to stoop when entering; but a more truthful explanation depends less on humility than on discouraging the Saracen horsemen.

Constantine's mosaic pavements can still be seen, despite Justinian's rebuilding which added an apse shaped like a trefoil; and on the heavy columns still remain the painted armorial crests and patron saints of the Crusader knights.

Before the Altar of the Nativity, narrow stairs descend to the candlelit Grotto where the event took place. Through the doorway of Crusader marble (and one can imagine their awe as they knelt in the holy place), the site of the Saviour's birth is visible, marked by a silver star set in the floor.

Like the Holy Sepulchre, the Church of the Nativity is shared by several denominations—Greek Orthodox, Armenian and

Latin (Franciscan)—each having chapels and altars within the complex. The Greek altar is dazzlingly rich, bedecked with silver and icons, and the Latin chapel is a more modern building adjoining the L-shaped Greek structure on the north side. At Christmas, Bethlehem holds its finest celebrations. There are great processions of the various denominations, the streets packed with onlookers, and the Latin choirs sing in Manger Square as the pilgrims enter for Mass or visit the Chapel of the Manger where Mary cradled the Christchild.

Bethlehem has its own distinctive life too. Like so many of the smaller Judean towns, it retains the air of a village. Its trucks slow down for the laden donkeys, its streets wind threadlike and busy with jostling life. And around it, beyond the fields were Ruth met Boaz, the hills of Judea reach across the open country toward the Dead Sea.

East of Bethlehem, among the caves of the early anchorites who settled in the desert, the monastery of Mar Saba nestles in the shelter of a steep ravine. St Sabas, who founded it, was a important theologian in the fifth century and the monastery became a centre of religious literature despite its isolated position. It may also have been used as a penal monastery, although the monks deny this and certainly its difficulty of access was, in the past, quite usual for these desert dwellings.

At one time, the monastic community was large and flourishing and, after its original foundation in the fifth century, the monastery became an important centre of literature and poetry, a tiny enclave of civilized learning in the midst of the desert. Its isolation, however, made it vulnerable to attack and it was sacked and reduced to ruin many times over the centuries. It was finally rebuilt in 1840, by the government of Imperial Russia—a fact hard to believe for, in its rockbound tranquillity, it has kept the atmosphere of its past. Surrounded by white-washed walls and courtyards, Mar Saba's church has a Byzantine splendour of ornamentation—gold and icons and intricate carved wood. The monks, aided in their daily chores by the local Bedouin, are hospitable and their small guest-room is a welcome refuge from the desert heat.

The Herodion was a refuge of a different kind, one of the chain of great fortresses built throughout Judea by King Herod. His feverish obsession with security led him to build the defensive walls 70 feet high, and from the 100-foot towers, his soldiers commanded a view of the country as far as Mount Scopus. Herod was buried in this fortress, according to the writings of the time, though his tomb has not yet been discovered; and either he or the Zealots made one of the inner rooms a synagogue. In the revolt against Rome, the Herodion was among the last of the fortresses to fall to the legions and it is thought that the defenders—like those at Masada—committed mass suicide rather than surrender.

To the south, the villages round Bethlehem, with their vineyards and their terraced fields, force the desert to give way. Near one such village, Artes off the Hebron road, are Solomon's Pools. The scarceness of water made it a doubly precious commodity in the area and the Mameluke Sultan Qualaun probably had good reason to build his fortress which still guards the ancient reservoirs. Their name is misleading and their association with the Biblical king is apocryphal, referring to a verse in the lovely Song of Solomon. It is more likely that the Pools were built in Roman times, when their waters flowed along Jerusalem's aqueducts— even today they form part of the city's water supply.

Many of the local Arab villagers 'commute' to a young township springing up to the right of the highway south. It adjoins the group of predominantly religious kibbutzim known as the Etzion Bloc. Some of its young members are the descendants of the original settlers who were killed when the kibbutzim were destroyed by the Arab Legion in the 1948 war, and the present settlements were rebuilt after 1967, when the site fell within Israeli-occupied territory.

From here, the Mediterranean is visible in the far distance although Hebron, a bare 10 miles away, is hidden in its shallow scoop of a valley. Hebron is the largest southernmost town before the Judean Wilderness runs into the Negev, and one of the major cities of the West Bank. It can also claim the somewhat odd distinction of being the only holy city of Israel whose mayor is an aristocratic Arab Sheikh. It has prospered since 1967, particularly in agriculture as more advanced methods and wider use of mechanized farming have taken the place of the old ways (though the Hebronites don't really concede that the improvement is due to Israeli administration). However that may be, Hebrew shop signs are gradually appearing among the Arabic, while Israeli commerce is slowly mingling with local enterprise—a process that is also taking place in the other West Bank towns.

Its recorded history goes back thousands of years. Hebron was one of the Canaanite strongholds conquered by the Israelites under Joshua and the Book of Numbers tells how Moses, obeying the word of God, sent men '... to spy out the land of Canaan, and said unto them, Get you up this way southward and go up into the mountain; And see the land what it is; ... whether it be fat or lean, whether there be wood therein or not. And be ye of good courage, and bring of the fruit of the land. ... So they went up and searched the land. ... And they ascended by the south and came to Hebron; ... (Now Hebron was built seven years before Zoan in Egypt)'. Zoan was founded in 1720 BC which makes Hebron very old indeed. After the Israelite conquest, it became the capital of the tribe of Judah—perhaps because of the encouraging news brought back by the spies, who returned laden with the fruit of the area. Even today, Hebron is famous for its grapes, many of which find their way to at least one nearby monastery—that of Cremizon at Beit Jallah, west of Bethleham—for the excellent wine that can be sampled free by any traveller. David had links with Hebron, as with Bethleham. 'In Hebron he reigned over Judah seven years and six months' before conquering the city he was to make his capital, 'and in Jerusalem he reigned thirty and three years over all Israel and Judah'.

But Hebron's major significance in religious history goes back even further—to the first of its numerous mentions in the Bible, concerning the nomadic Patriarch, Abraham. Here, he pitched his tents '... in the plain of Mamre, which is in Hebron, and built there an altar unto the Lord.' (Genesis 13:18). And in Hebron too, he bought the cave of Machpela as a burial site for his family and himself.

Three of the Patriarchs and their wives are buried there—Abraham and Sarah, Isaac and Rebecca, and Jacob and Leah. (Reference has already been made to the tomb of Rachel, Jacob's second wife, and Jewish tradition does not accord with the Muslim belief that Joseph too is buried in Machpela.) With the burial of the Patriarchs, the cave became a venerated Jewish site, holier than any but the Western Wall of the Temple in Jerusalem. And, again like the Temple, it is a Muslim shrine that stands on the site, the Mosque of Ibrahim. Muhamed revered the Jewish Patriarchs, regarding them also as prophets of the faith of Islam. The Muslims call Abraham al-Khalil, the Friend (of the Lord) and the mosque is also known as the Haram, 'Sanctuary'.

The Herodian walls around the mosque are impressively well-preserved and stand at almost their original height. The lower part is 10 solid feet thick, bearing an upper row of pillars. Inside the mosque, it is shaded and peaceful, and the glare of the street becomes a dim, rich dusk. Muslim decoration habitually uses Koranic quotations and the Arabic script ornaments the rooms where the cenotaphs of the Patriarchs stand, covered with gold-embroidered cloth. The cenotaphs are of delicately-coloured marble and, in the presence of such ancient holiness, it is impossible to resist a feeling of awe, though the traditional burial places are far below, in the caves underneath the hill on which the mosque is built.

Outside the town, the villages fan out sparsely and the doors of their houses are painted green to keep off the evil eye. The wilderness stretches as far as the road along the Dead Sea's western shore which leads past Qumran to Jericho. The water is salt, and so buoyant that sinking is impossible; but, hundreds of feet above, a clear freshwater spring feeds not only modern Israel's loveliest natural swimming pool, but an oasis that existed in Biblical times and now sustains the kibbutz of the same name, Ein Gedi, the 'fountain of the kid'.

'And it came to pass, when Saul was returned from following the Philistines, that it was told him, saying, Behold David is in the wilderness of En-gedi.' The bleak country surrounding the oasis was where David took refuge from Saul. The first Book of Samuel goes on to relate how Saul searched for David in a cave; how, under cover of the darkness that kept him safe, David crept up and tore Saul's robe, offering it to him as a token of his affection, '... for in that I cut off the skirt of thy robe and killed thee not, know thou and see that there is neither evil nor transgression in mine hand and I have not sinned against thee;'. And thereafter, the oasis' spring was named for David, his Fountain.

The oasis' grapes must have been famous even then for they were spoken of the Song of Solomon, 'My beloved is unto me as a cluster of camphire in the vineyards of En-gedi.' The love-song's praise is also an apt reference. The kibbutz's grapes and peaches are among the earliest of the season's produce to appear in the market. The area is a nature reserve and one of its most charming sights is that of the wild deer who come down from the Judean hills to drink and rest in the shady grounds of the natural history museum.

The settlement's past in Israelite times was unearthed by the excavation of Tel Goren; and a temple and sacred enclosure date back to the Chalcolithic period, millenia before. A synagogue and Roman bath lie at the foot of the tel and Ein Gedi's prominence during the second Temple is indicated by further finds, including a number in the region of the nearby Hever Valley.

One of the most famous archaeological discoveries of the present day was that of the Dead Sea Scrolls at Qumran, north of Ein Gedi. The manner in which they were found has almost the ring of a fairy-tale; the young shepherd boy (echoes of David) searching for a lost lamb and finding instead the marvellous fragments.

The Scrolls were written on papyrus and their remarkable preservation within their goatskin wrappings was due to the dryness of the atmosphere of the region. They related to a Jewish sect, the Essenes, who maintained a settlement at Qumran at the time of Christ. This is significant because it was an era of fierce religious factionalism and the Essenes were just one of many dissident sects who went their own way during the general turmoil. They were ascetic and pious, and adhered strictly to their own exalted interpretation of the Law. They rejected the Hasmonean priesthood for the authority of their own priests, for example, and they kept their own festivals at variance with the normal Jewish holy days. They believed that they were the 'Chosen of the Lord', and that those who were not perished forever. They believed also in the apocalypse, symbolized by the war between the 'Sons of Light and the Sons of Darkness'—with the Sons of Light ultimately victorious. They placed great importance on ritual purification by water and their skills were renowned in the fields of medicine and astrology. The scrolls which gave this picture of their community were found in the caves of the cliffs along the shore; and a painstaking excavation revealed the buildings of the settlement, the 'monastery', with its numerous rooms for different purposes (though many members lived outside its walls). Despite its destruction by the Romans in the great revolt of the first century, Qumran's remains and the Essene writings provide a fascinating view of the nation's past.

North of Qumran, the road leads away from the Dead Sea towards Jericho. The usual route is from Jerusalem but either way crosses the 'lost world' landscape of the Jordan Valley against which the first glimpse of Jericho's greenness comes almost as a shock. The city is an oasis, its citrus groves and palm trees thriving arrogantly in the face of the desert. For a time at least, the nagging old spiritual about Jericho is driven from mind, though it returns later when one visits the tel of the prehistoric city that stands near the Ein es-Sultan, the pool of Elisha where the prophet made the waters sweet.

'Modern' Jericho still bears the signs of its splendid past when the Umayyad caliphs wintered here in its delightful climate. The ruins of their palaces show the opulence with which the court surrounded itself when it left Damascus' colder air to travel south. Most of the frescoes and ornaments of the palace at Khirbet Mafjir are now in the Rockefeller Museum in Jerusalem but, among the ruins, the marvellous mosaics of the royal bath-house —the tessellated 'Tree of Life'—still gleam brilliantly, a reminder of the reputation of the early caliphs as patrons of the arts.

7,000 years of Jericho's past (perhaps more) lie under the northern tel, as yet only partly excavated. Some authorities believe it may be as much as 10,000 years old, older even than Damascus. It had walls and towers in Neolithic times, in the eighth millenium BC, compared to which the Roman and Byzantine remains around the tel can be seen, perhaps, in a different perspective of antiquity.

'And the Lord said unto Joshua, See, I have given into thine hand Jericho. . . .' The jingling spiritual comes back more strongly than ever and its first verse ends with the nub of the matter. The walls did, indeed, 'come tumblin' down'. But why? The Book of Joshua describes the miraculous event more fully. 'And ye shall compass the city, all ye men of war, and go round about the city once. Thus shalt thou do six days. And seven priests shall bear before the ark seven trumpets of rams' horns: and the seventh day ye shall compass the city seven times, and the priests shall blow with the trumpets. And it shall come to pass, that when they make a long blast with the ram's horn, and when ye hear the sound of the trumpet, all the people shall shout with a great shout; and the wall of the city shall fall down flat. . . .' As a great writer has pointed out, miracles often happen by non-miraculous means, and although no absolute evidence has yet been forthcoming to explain the event, it is perhaps possible that the walls, weighted with age, were finally destroyed by the vibration.

Away from the tel and the Umayyad elegance, Jericho is a

modern West Bank city. Its climate still makes it a popular winter resort (though for Jerusalem now, not Damascus) and its open air restaurants and gardens make it a pleasant day-trip. For the same reason, its agriculture flourishes and its winter vegetables find a ready market. The refugee camps on the outskirts of the city are mostly empty, the former occupants now living either in Israel or Jordan although a fraction returned to the camps. More of their population went to the vocational training centre on the Jerusalem highway to learn technological skills while they lived there.

The slow integration of Israeli and Arab commerce again manifests itself in the shop signs, the trucks, the advertisements. Some of the large Israeli stores are opening branches in Jericho too. The 'open bridges' policy maintained by Israel since the six-day War is still in effect though with tighter security, for obvious reasons, since the war in 1973. The Allenby Bridge is used daily by a constant flow of traffic each way carrying students, visiting relatives, workers—and the West Bank fruit and vegetables for Jordanian consumption.

Beyond Jericho, Samaria stretches north towards the Galilee. The road from Jerusalem to Nablus passes Ramallah on the way and cuts right through the centre of the region parallel to the invisible border that divides the desert to the east from the agricultural land lying to the west.

Samaria derives its name from the ancient capital of the seceding tribes of Israel when the kingdom split in two after Solomon's death. The city of Samaria was founded in the ninth century BC by Omri, most powerful of the northern kings. It was a violent kingdom of bitter dynastic rivalries and frequent changes of ruler—in contrast with the southern state of Judah which retained Jerusalem as its capital and, the Davidic dynasty for its monarchs. Under Omri and his successor, Ahab, Samaria was opened to the ennervating luxury of the Phoenician civilization. The ensuing internal disputes caused by this further weakened the kingdom and it fell to the Assyrians a century and a half later. Most of the Israelites were exiled and Babylonian exiles were imported in turn to take their place and the Babylonian-Israelite descendants became the race known as the Samaritans, of later fame. The city's fortunes varied over the centuries until it enjoyed another period of glory under Herod. To flatter his Roman masters, he renamed the city Sebaste (Sebastos is Greek for Augustus), raising a temple in honour of the emperor and carrying out major rebuilding programmes which employed his unquestioned talents as an administrator to the utmost.

The city is still impressive, even in its ruins. Herod's amphitheatre and colonnaded streets, the great pillars and the basilica erected by a later emperor, crown the hilltop looking out over the Samarian countryside in all directions.

Its closest neighbour is some 10 miles away. Nablus, the ancient Shechem, is today the most heavily-populated and modern of the West Bank cities. Its name, indeed, means 'new city', for it was originally called Neapolis when Vespasian founded it in the first century. Its prosperity comes from a number of thriving light industries and from agriculture. It is also well-known for its excellent soap which sells throughout the West Bank and in Israel.

Its ancient counterpart, Shechem, was yet another of the Canaanite cities that fell to the Israelites although, because of the friendly relations that apparently existed between the two, no great effort was needed. It is located at the eastern entrance to Nablus and the mountains on either side are those of which Moses spoke to the Israelite tribes when he commanded them, on entering the Promised Land, to offer up on Mt Gerizim a blessing and on Mt Ebal a curse.

The Samaritans have a particular connection with Gerizim in that it is their holy mountain. Incensed by the refusal of the returned Babylonian exiles to let them share the reconstruction

11 Donkey transport in Nazareth Bazaar

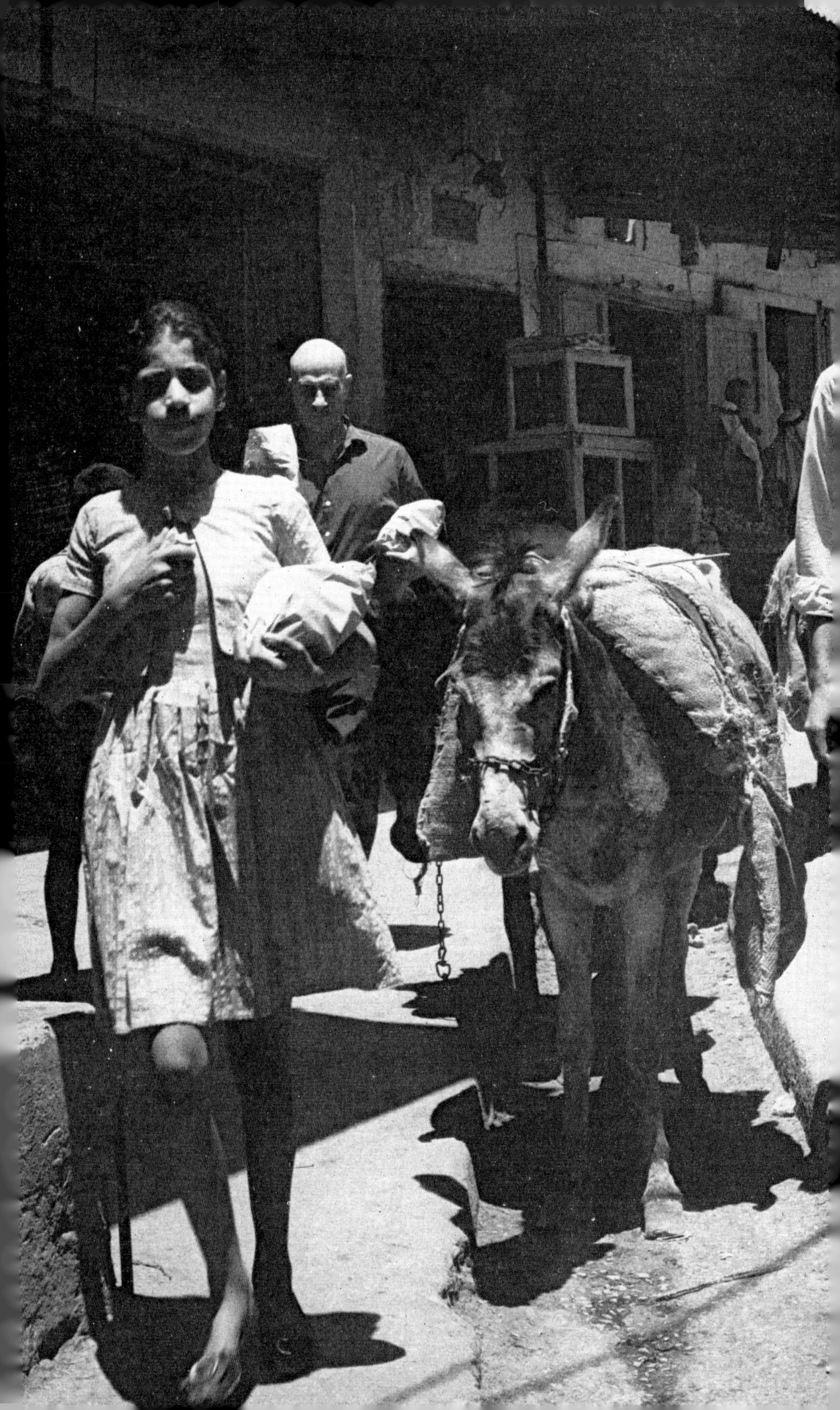

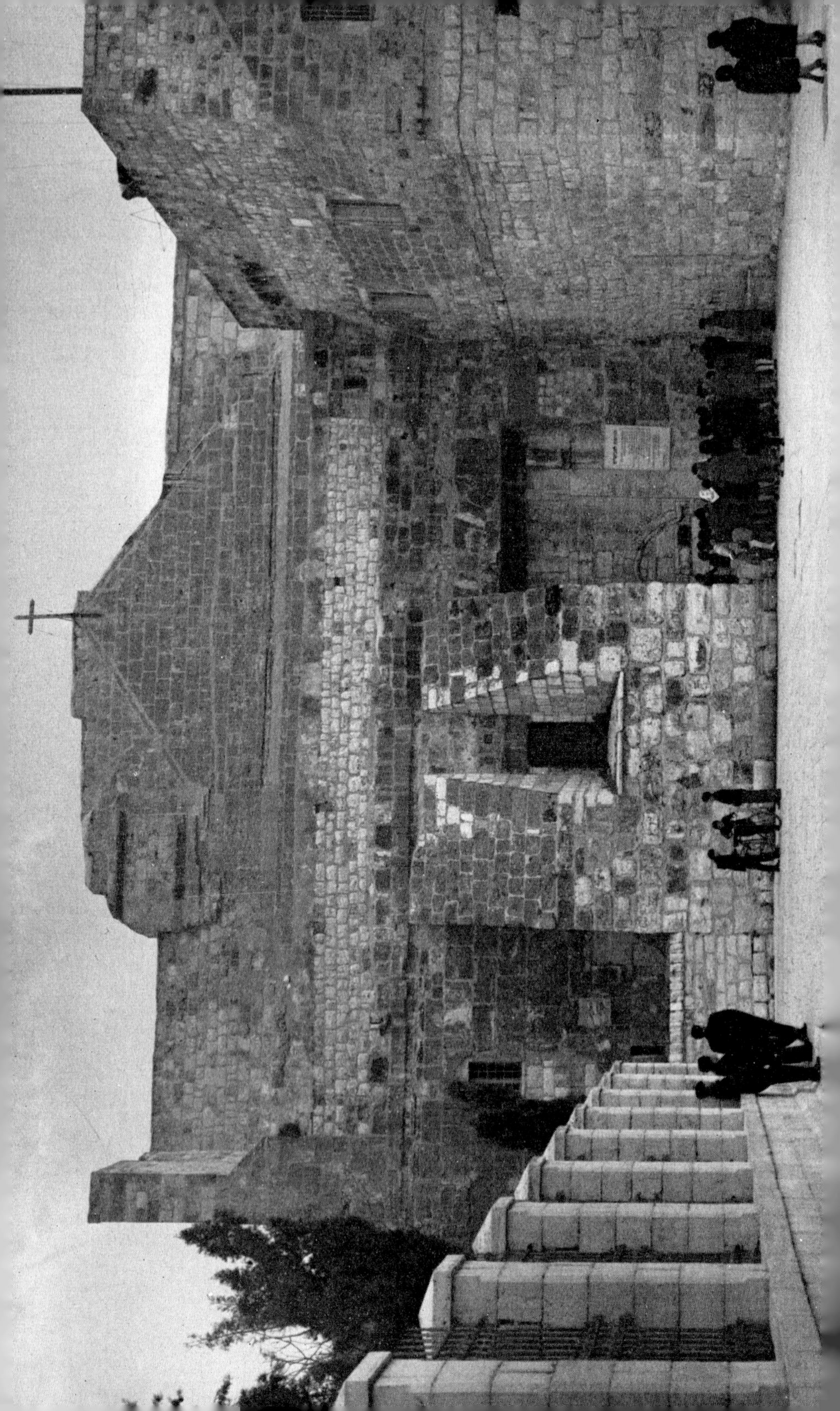

of the Temple, the Samaritans established their own spiritual centre at Gerizim in defiance of Jerusalem. Today, the sect numbers a mere handful, part of whose members live around Nablus and part near Tel Aviv. They celebrate Passover on the mountain and, of the Old Testament, recognize only the Five Books of Moses.

Shechem is repeatedly mentioned in the Bible in connection with the Israelites and the bones of Joseph, brought from Egypt with the Exodus, were buried here.

On its way south to Jerusalem, the road passes Shiloh where the Ark of the Covenant rested from the time of Judges to that of Samuel, and where the tribe of Benjamin went to seek the 'daughters of Shiloh'. A little way before Ramallah, a detour leads to the village of Beitin. It is the Beth-El of the Bible, the 'House of God' where Abraham built an altar to the Lord after He had shown him the Promised Land. It is also the place where the Lord appeared to Jacob as he dreamed, and promised him '... the land whereon thou liest, to thee will I give it, and to thy seed; ...' When Jacob awoke, he took the stone he had used for a pillow and raised it as a pillar, 'And he called the name of that place Beth-el'.

Ramallah is Arabic for 'Height of God'. It is an apt name, for this pleasant town lies nearly 3,000 feet high in the mountains and its cool dry air made it as popular a resort in summer as Jericho in winter. The large affluent villas that line the road to Jerusalem serve as expensive holiday residences for wealthy Arabs although the town itself is predominantly Christian. Jerusalem is some 12 miles off but its northern boundary has stretched like a piece of elastic nearly as far as Ramallah in order to contain the new Atarot airport at Kalandiyah. The airport, which already connects Jerusalem with north and south Israel—Eilat, Tel Aviv and Rosh Pina—is being rapidly modernized and expanded to receive direct flights from the States and Europe and take much of the load now

12 Bethlehem: the Church of the Nativity

carried solely by Lod (now Ben Gurion) Airport. A large new industrial estate is springing up nearby, providing work both for new immigrants and the local Arab population.

Approaching Jerusalem's suburbs, Nebi Samwil becomes visible on the right, the traditional site of the burial of the Prophet Samuel. The mosque here stands on high ground and from its minaret medieval pilgrims would catch their first sight of Jerusalem—from which derived its Latin title of Mons Gaudii, 'Mount of Joy'.

6. Galilee

The Galilee's hills and valleys tumble southward from Mount Hermon and the furthermost town, Metullah (in uncomfortable proximity to the Lebanese border), to the Jezreel Valley, the 'granary of Israel'. Down its eastern side runs the Jordan with Syria beyond, and to the west it reaches the Mediterranean. It is a rich land—in its crops, in its beauty and in its history—and it has known many peoples and many cultures. Ancient battles were fought here by the heroes whose names—Joshua, Barak, Deborah—resound in the Bible. Christ first preached in the synagogues of Galilee and made his converts from the fishermen on its lake. The great scholars and mystics of Judaism lived here and studied and, of the four holy cities of Israel, two are in Galilee—Safed and Tiberias. More recently, its revival after the long Turkish stagnation was brought about, begun by the pioneers of the last century. To their painstaking labours was later added modern technology and, with the possible exception of the citrus-groves of the Sharon, the Galilee is now the most abundantly productive region in the country, as well as one of the most beautiful.

It is a hilly region dividing geographically into three areas. Upper Galilee embraces the Hula Valley, the ancient town of Safed and the northern shore of Lake Tiberias. It has the disadvantage of bordering the Golan Heights and the advantage of being particularly fortunate in its water resources, several tributaries joining with the Banias river—supplied by the melting snows of Mt Hermon—to flow into the Jordan. The ancient northern border of Israel stood here, the Biblical town of Dan whose river of the same name is one of the Jordan's tributaries. Kiryat Shmona, a flourishing small industrial town a few miles south, is as young as Dan is old but already has a history of its own. Shmona means 'eight'—the eight young men and women who, under their leader, Josef Trumpeldor, died holding the nearby colony of Tel Hai, 'Hill of Life', against Arab marauders— still an occupational hazard of the smaller settlements and border towns.

This is the tip of the Hula, the farming valley and nature reserve that presents some of the most beautiful landscapes in Israel. Once a lake stood here, but it was drained for reclamation for agriculture. The small remaining marshland is a sanctuary for the vast flocks of migratory birds that visit each year—wild geese, ducks, pelicans and even more exotic varieties. Fish are also plentiful, probably the most useful variety being an imported breed which feeds on the eggs of the malarial mosquitoes that were once a major hazard. Now, however, malaria has completely disappeared like the blackwater fever that the early settlers had also to contend with as they tackled the eroded topsoil and drained the swamps (described by Josephus in Roman times as a feature of the area).

The reclamation of the valley from its picturesque desolation began as far back as 1878. Over the next few years, the settlement of Rosh Pina was established—the highway now passes it on the way to Tiberias—and others followed, helped in their precarious but willing efforts by Baron de Rothschild. Despite this, many of them failed but the First World War saw an influx of pioneers with fresh enthusiasm, who backed up their idealism with the agricultural and manual skills needed for success. They fought disease and deprivation, local Arabs raiders and their own inexperience and ignorance. In the early 1930s, the Palestine Land Development Company bought the right to reclaim 10,000 waterlogged acres. With the coming of independence, the concessions were handed over to the Jewish National Fund, the agency responsible for land development, which has since reclaimed over 200,000 acres by drainage and tree-planting, working through the Hula Valley Authority to make the neglected regions once more habitable.

Hula's swamps were found to have been caused by the deflection of the course of the Jordan as a result of age-old volcanic eruptions. In order to dry out the swampland the river would have to be re-routed—and it was. The mammoth task was begun in 1951 and took seven years to complete, the ancient obstructions being removed by the building of a series of canals, dams and culverts. 'Swamp-thickets' of papyrus had to be uprooted although this rare vegetation has found a sanctuary, like the birds, in the nature reserve. The rewards of this gigantic and costly enterprise are the rich new farmlands whose crops—cotton and groundnuts, maize and melons, flowers and a variety of vegetables—offer record yields. Rapidly multiplying villages and small farming communities now thrive in the valley.

Apropos of water, one other great development project deserves mention. The project was based on the fact that while the eastern Galilee had too much water, the Negev desert had too little. After draining the swamp, the Israelis decided to water the desert and the plan, begun in the 1960s, was designed to carry over 300 million cubic metres of water annually a distance of 150 miles. The diversion of the Jordan, not unnaturally perhaps, aroused Jordanian objections. The dispute was finally solved when Jordan, the country most affected, carried out diversion of a tributary of the Jordan river while Israel continued with its own development, pumping water out of Lake Tiberias.

Hula is a region connected also with the ancient Israelites— the tribes who came out of the desert to conquer the cities of Canaan. The tel of Hazor, one of those cities, stands near the kibbutz Ayelet Hashahar. This is the site of the ancient city whose king fought with Joshua. A recent excavation unearthed many finds from successive layers of civilization and some are exhibited in a museum near the kibbutz though most of them, being so important, can be found in Jerusalem's Archaeological Museum. Hazor was mentioned as long ago as 1900 BC in the list of cities who rebelled against Egypt's domination. Joshua captured it, Solomon levied taxes on its people to fortify its strongholds and build the Temple. A few centuries later, it fell to the Assyrians and centuries later still, the Maccabees fought for its possession before the city finally fell into decay.

A city with a different kind of history is Hazor's neighbour, Safed. Safed's past is associated with the things of the spirit, with mysticism and the esoteric teachings of the Kabbalists. It is one of the four holy cities, a beautiful town climbing the hillside nearly 3,000 feet above sea level, and in the purity of its air, the mystics felt close to God. It has an almost magical remoteness, a feeling of other-wordliness which lingers in its narrow streets, its low Arab houses and dim-lit synagogues. Its charm is enhanced by a thriving colony of artists who live and work here—their annual Purim carnival is delightful. During the early part of the sixteenth century, Safed became the most important Jewish centre on the Holy Land, a refuge for many of those driven out of Spain in 1492 by Ferdinand and Isabella. The finest scholars and rabbis gathered round Rabbi Isaac Luria, himself a devout admirer of the great Rabbi Shimon ben Yochai who is said to have compiled the Kabbala centuries before. Rabbi Luria's own teachings were compiled in the 'Shulchan Aruch', written by a disciple and codifying religious practice for Jewish daily life. Rabbi ben Yochai was a fugitive from Roman oppression and lived, together with his son, in a cave at Peki'in. His tomb is five miles outside Safed at Mount Meron. Orthodox Jews regard it as a holy place and visit it annually on the festival of Lag B'Omer to pay homage, and to dance and chant throughout the night.

From one holy city to another, Tiberias, the landscape along the way is fittingly beautiful as the hills slope down to Kinneret. Lake Kinneret lies nearly 700 feet below sea level and a well-endowed imagination may see in its shape the 'harp' which is the English meaning of its Hebrew name. It is variously called Lake

Tiberias or the Sea of Galilee and around its placid shores, the scene is still reminiscent of the time of Christ with fishermen and their boats and the nets drying in the sun. It was on these waters that He walked, one of the sudden storms of the lake that He calmed; and, of course, it was the fishermen of the lake, Simon and Andrew, his brother, who became His first disciples, instructed to become 'fishers of men'.

The city lies on Kinneret's western shore. Named after an emperor, it was founded by Herod Antipas in the year AD 19 as a city in the Roman mould, even to the building of that most Roman of institutions, a hippodrome. The Pharisees and orthodox Jews were disgusted and outraged, and Christ avoided the city as he travelled and taught around the lake. It became a holy city with the establishment of the Sanhedrin, the Jewish priestly court, when the destruction of the Temple caused the centre of Jewish cultural and spiritual life to move from Jerusalem to the Galilee. The scholars and rabbis who settled in Tiberias completed with loving effort the Jerusalem, or Palestinian, Talmud, and the town gradually sloughed off its earlier bad name. Until the fourth century, it was entirely Jewish except for the Roman garrisons. Even when the Byzantines and, later, the Muslims, brought their faiths, their mosques and churches to Tiberias, it remained a peaceful corner of the Galilee. In fact, everything about Tiberias seems peaceful, including its landscape and its exceptional climate. It served as a winter resort of the Caesars for this very reason and the warm springs to the south of the city were famous even in those days.

The great philosopher, Maimonides, is buried in the city and the famous Rabbi Akiba (who died fighting the Roman occupation) is also said to have been buried here although the tomb is apocryphal.

It is possible to explore Tiberias pleasantly on foot and, if the attractions of history prove too crowded, the lake gives some of the best water-skiing in the country. On the opposite shore, the enterprising kibbutz of Ein Gev provides a superb lunch of lake-caught fish (and the ferry to reach it. The trip takes a leisurely hour and if you prefer to swim, there is an annual 5-mile race across the lake). Ein Gev has a delightful music festival each year which attracts some of the world's finest musicians. So popular did it prove that a large modern auditorium had to be built to house it—a fine achievement by any standards and especially so when contrasted with the settlement's precarious beginnings in an exposed and isolated position which suffered constantly from enemy attacks. 'And Jesus went about all Galilee. . . .' The road along the northern shore of Lake Tiberias is a journey through the New Testament. Thousands of pilgrims annually visit the Mount of Beatitudes, Taghba and Capernaum, for their revered associations with Christ's teachings. (Such a journey would take in the rather nondescript village of Migdal north of Tiberias, the Magdala of ancient times and birthplace of Mary Magdalen.)

The Mount of Beatitudes is worth climbing just for the view. It rises over 300 feet above the lake, crowned by a Franciscan hospice kept by nuns, and a chapel decorated with the signs of the seven virtues. Safed hugs the mountainside in the distance and beyond it, Hermon's snow is bright in the sun. On the mount by tradition, Jesus chose his apostles. . . .' And he goeth up into a mountain and calleth unto him whom he would. . . . And he ordained twelve . . . that he might send them forth to preach, And to have power to heal sicknesses and to cast out devils'. The devils were cast out by Jesus himself at Capernaum, where he lived when he came from Nazareth . . . 'and they went into Capernaum and straightway on the Sabbath day he entered in the synagogue and taught'. Its Hebrew name was Kfar Nahum and in the grounds of a Franciscan monastery stands a second-century synagogue, one of the loveliest in Galilee, which was probably built over the one in which Jesus preached when he made Capernaum the 'centre of his teaching' and healed the sick.

At Taghba, to the south, the miracle of the loaves and fishes took place and on this site the Benedictines built a monastery of native stone. In the remains of a Byzantine church, splendid mosaics depict the miracle in a lovely setting of Galilee's fauna. Not far from Taghba are the prehistoric caves of Nahal Amud where excavations have unearthed the paleolithic Skull of Galilee, over 100,000 years old.

The history of the Crusaders in the Holy Land is one of dedication, greed and bloodshed. Karnei Hittin, the 'Horns of the Hittite', stands as a monument to their battle with Islam for the control of Palestine. Their defeat by Saladin in 1187 put an end to the brief dominance of Christianity, although the Crusader presence lingered for another century before it faded out and the Cross took its banners elsewhere. At the hill's foot is the tomb of Jethro, the father-in-law of Moses, venerated by the Druse as a prophet. Their pilgrimage and festival takes place each spring across the Arbel Valley where, it is said, the Messiah will come. In Herod's reign, the Jewish resistance fighters hid in the many caves that pierced the cliffs at the edge of the plain, the legionaries being lowered to the caves in baskets to smoke them out.

At the southern tip of the lake is Deganya, 'the mother of the kibbutzim'. Set in fertile acres with citrus orchards, banana groves and vineyards, it is one of the most charming of settlements despite its vulnerable position which caused it to be hard-hit by the Syrian and Iraqui forces who invaded the area during the 1948 war and were driven off by the determined resistance of the kibbutzniks.

The Jordan Valley continues its way south to the Dead Sea, bisected initially by the road to Beth Shean. On the heights overlooking both road and valley stands the great fortress of Belvoir, its massive walls raised by the Hospitallers near the end of the twelfth century. Unlike Montfort in western Galilee which was built about 50 years later by the Teutonic Knights to house their archives and was, therefore, strategically unimportant, Belvoir dominated the entire countryside with a commanding outlook to the hills on the far side of the valley. Under Saracen attack, it remained in possession of the Order and was one of the last strongholds to fall after the battle of Hattin.

Beth Shean also lies close to the Jordan, in the Harod Valley. In ancient times, it was a Canaanite stronghold although most of the finds unearthed by excavation were taken elsewhere, only a few remaining to be displayed in the museum. It is also associated with the moving death of Saul. The Old Testament relates, '(the Philistines) found Saul and his three sons fallen on mount Gilboa ... and they fastened his body to the wall of Beth-Shan'. The bodies were taken down by night by the men of Gilead to be buried with the honours befitting their dead leader. During the Hellenistic craze that swept the Holy Land after the death of Alexander, the city was renamed Scythopolis and achieved fame in later centuries as the site of Christ's healing of the leper. Possibly the most important of later finds is the Roman theatre. Built in the second century, this impressive piece of architecture is one of the best-preserved of its type in the Near East.

Between Beth Shean and the sea lies the Jezreel Valley, the granary of Israel. It is also known as the Vale of Esdraelon, or simply as the Emek, 'valley', (although emek is used—without a capital letter—throughout the Galilee to denote any plain or valley). The Arabs called it the Gateway to Hell, perhaps a reference to the malaria-ridden swamps and marshes that made it uninhabitable until the early settlers, mainly from eastern Europe in the Third Aliyah, changed it over the decades into the richest farmland in Israel.

'Aliyah' is one of the emotive words in Israeli political development, which can only be understood by its translation—immigration. Formed from the Hebrew verb 'to climb', it symbolizes the rebirth of the nation, the return of people scattered in alien societies, who sought to search and rebuild their lost identities in their own homeland. The 'Third Aliyah', coming mainly from Russia (and including many of today's well known politicians), was the first conscious and organized effort to return groups of immigrants from Eastern Europe to Palestine. It is a concept that not only points to a significant stage in Israel's history but also designates a particular approach to the way in which the building of a land was to be undertaken.

Geologically, the valley was formed by a subsidence in the earth's surface causing numerous springs to appear which provided the basis for human settlement. Passages through the valley were opened up, adding to its strategic importance in later centuries and making a desirable prize for any would-be invader – of which there were many. The empires that conquered the Holy Land fought also in the Galilee for this great natural trade route between Africa and Mesopotamia.

In the Emek, though, the present is more important than the past, and its inhabitants more interested in planting than in fighting. The neglected and desolate areas of the Mameluke centuries have disappeared and so have the Bedouin who once grazed their sheep here. Until the end of the nineteenth century, the land belonged almost to absentee landlords and remained sadly uncultivated. The land purchases of the early 1900s by the Jewish National Fund not only brought willing hands and dedicated labour but made possible those explorations into communal living and farming, the kibbutz and the moshav; and in the renewal of the land despite all the hardships, the self-respect of a downtrodden people was also renewed.

From land reclamation and the efforts of the pioneers, the Galilee went on to town planning and modern industry. In the 1960s, the development of Galilee was Israel's largest rural planning programme, aiding the establishment or enlargement of villages and urban centres throughout the area, based on a principle of pooled resources and activities in every major field. The new settlers, whether from Europe or North Africa (the latter in particular found life very different from that in their countries of origin), adapted well both to the living conditions and the work in new towns such as Carmiel and Nahariya. The first is in the hills of inland Galilee and the second has become perhaps its best-known coastal resort. Nahariya was originally settled by German Jews in 1934. Many were urban intellectuals who, in a classic example of adaptability, turned their hand to tourism with extremely successful results.

The villages and settlements are now able to add industrial plants to their agricultural holdings, integrating them into the area's farming operations. At Ein-Harod, for example, citrus packing and crop processing are carried on for the whole district as part of the activities of an industrial complex.

Ein Harod stands in the lower corner of Galilee, where Jezreel runs towards Jordan. Nearby is the stream where Gideon's 300 warriors were chosen to fight the Midianites, those that '... lapped, putting their hand to their mouth', as told in the Book of Judges. Ein Harod has two excellent museums, one archaeological and the other displaying local Israeli arts.

From the centre of the Emek, all roads lead to Afula. Although a rather unimpressive town, the highways that connect it with all the central towns as far as the coast, reflect its importance as the crossroads of the trade routes of the country. Nowadays, it is the market town for the whole valley, dominated by its newer half, Afula Ilit, on the hill to the north. Old Afula was briefly distinguished by Bonaparte, when he used it as a base for his attack against the Turks in the Battle of Mount Tabor. Tabor, in fact, stands 15 miles further north. It rises impressively to a height of nearly 2,000 feet and the steep climbing road requires some motoring skill, but the view from its summit is superb, revealing the landscape stretching from Kinneret to Carmel. Tabor's history reaches back to the Israelite conquest of Canaan, when one of the judges was Deborah the prophetess 'and the children of Israel came up to her for judgement'. Here, she gathered the northern tribes together under Barak, her general, to do battle against the Canaanites because 'the Lord sold them (the children of Israel) into the hand of Jabin, king of Canaan, that reigned in Hazor; the captain of whose host was Sisera ... and the children of Israel cried unto the Lord; for he had nine hundred chariots of iron; and twenty years he mightily oppressed the children of Israel'.

Galilee 121

In the fourth century, Tabor aroused Christian interest when St Cyril claimed it as the site of the Transfiguration (formerly thought to be Mt Hermon). Successive centuries saw the claim established with the building of numerous churches and a Byzantine basilica on the site of the Transfiguration. The Franciscans have built a monastery and a hospice (from which the view is enchanting) near the remains of a Benedictine monastery on the Catholic section of the plateau. Adjoining its northern side, the Greek monastery of Mar Elias stands, on the site of a Byzantine church whose paved mosaic and apses still remain.

'Can there any good thing come out of Nazareth?' Nathanael asked of Philip. The reply was 'Come and see' as Philip took him to the carpenter's son. Jesus grew to manhood in Nazareth, and lived there until his baptism by John. The town is his shrine, its holiest place the cave where the angel brought to Mary the message of God, the Annunciation, of Jesus' birth. So it was said—the site, like so many others in the Holy Land, is perhaps doubtful and, again like other shrines, this matters less than the veneration and the faith of believers. Such faith was sufficient to erect, over the centuries, several churches to commemorate the event of the Annunciation—Byzantine, Crusader and Franciscan. The new basilica stands where the previous church was demolished (in 1954), partly on the site of the magnificent structure raised by the Crusaders, which was ruined by Baybars. The gaunt and beautiful capitals of the Crusader columns still stand; the cave beneath has an ancient altar, bearing the inscription, 'And the Word was made flesh'. In one of the sad conflicts that seem to arise so often in these matters, the Greek Orthodox sect maintains that its Church of St Gabriel is the true site. The original was a round church, built by Greek Christians who did not recognize the authority of the Pope, by the Fountain of Mary. The Greek claim is based on the Apocrypha of St James though the church, now entirely rebuilt, no longer encloses the Fountain from which Jesus and Mary drew water.

The word Nazareth has strong links with the Hebrew name for

Christians, 'notzrim' and certainly the Christian inhabitants are in the majority, although it is the largest Arab town in the country. Pilgrims of all denominations flock here to visit the shrines and the many churches, staying at the various hospices specially built for them, and at monasteries. Like many other old towns in Israel, it has its new section. Nazrat Ilit stands above it to the north east, modern, lively and bustling.

The road north leads to Kinneret, passing on the way a small, drab village which any traveller would be tempted to overlook but for the fact that this is Kafr Kana, the ancient Cana where Jesus turned water into wine. The Roman Catholic church claims that the ancient wine jars displayed in its crypt are the six waterpots mentioned in the Biblical story and that the church itself stands on the site of the house where the miracle occurred. It is built on the foundations of a Crusader church which in turn was built over a chapel of Constantine from the fourth century. The Greek Orthodox church, which has some fine interior decoration, is also claimed to stand on the site, displaying winejars that are of great antiquity, but probably of a later era. Whatever claim one believes, the story is told in the gospel of John as 'This beginning of miracles' done by Jesus.

On the road to Nazareth, some ten miles from Haifa, lies the subterranean city of Beit She'arim, the 'House of Gates'. It developed after the Romans had destroyed Jerusalem, Galilee becoming the centre of Jewish community life until the end of the Byzantine occupation. With Jerusalem in alien hands, the traditional cemetery on the Mount of Olives could not be used. The limestone rock of the Beit She'arim mountain proved to be suitable for tunnelling and thus the subterranean burial ground was established there. Remote and peaceful, it was a fitting place of rest for the Galilean rabbis and scholars. It became well known and wealthy Jews came there from far. The underground city was destroyed in AD 350. Today the mountainside has been cleared and the burial chambers are visited by tourists and scholars alike.

The walls bear Hebrew, Arabic and Greek inscriptions and, in spite of the Biblical law forbidding graven images, there are drawings of Biblical scenes and motifs such as Noah's Ark, the Lion of Judah and even Zeus, carved in stone.

Guarding western Jezreel stands the hill of Meggido, one of the most fascinating archaeological sites in the Holy Land. A fortress since ancient times, it has never ceased to be of strategic importance, as the key to the valley and the passage through the Galilee. Solomon kept his garrisons there and fortified the site. A king of Judah was killed there resisting the advance of the Egyptian king (who had no quarrel with him). It was at Megiddo that General Allenby broke through the Turkish lines in 1918 and, 30 years later, the Arab push toward Haifa was halted during the War of Independence.

Meggido, or Har Megiddon, became the Armageddon of St John, battlefield of the world's last struggle between Good and Evil (Revelations 16:16); and, of the conflicts that did take place in the past, the excavations of the 1920s and 30s revealed no fewer than 20 different strata, each one the ruin of a city rebuilt on its predecessor. The remains include those of Solomon's time, notably the king's stables and the irrigation system planned to withstand siege—an intricate feat of engineering. The oldest ruins, dating to about 4,000 BC, are the Canaanite temples. The commanding position that made Megiddo archaeologically rich has also provided it with a magnificent view of the valley from the top of the hill, which is deservedly famous.

7. Tel Aviv

Tel Aviv is in many ways an exasperating city (and in a country that often shows a highly exasperating stubbornness in its determination to survive, this is something of a compliment!) Its parent city, Yafo, is as old as Jerusalem but, not content with these venerable purlieus, in 1909 a group of citizens decided to establish a new quarter and settle it as a suburb of Yafo. They chose an unpromising cluster of sand dunes to the north, and Tel Aviv was born. Today, it is one of the three major cities of Israel, the other two being Haifa and Jerusalem, compared to both of which it is an infant, less than 70 years old. It is brash and boisterous with a longing for sophistication that shows itself in the multi-storey blocks, the hotels and discothèques; and it has a rate of development that leaves one slightly dizzy when contemplating it. It is, in a word, a microcosm of everything Israeli.

Long before the tourist trade began searching out every scrap of sun-drenched sand it could find, it sprawled unattractively along the Mediterranean, its hard-working inhabitants too busy to care about anything but its survival. Its site had none of the breath-taking grandeur of Haifa bay, rising up the sides of Carmel from the curving shoreline. It had no religious significance like Jerusalem, nor had it anything of great interest to the archaeologist or historian. In summer, the heat was oppressive, the air

13   Tel Aviv: Carmel Market

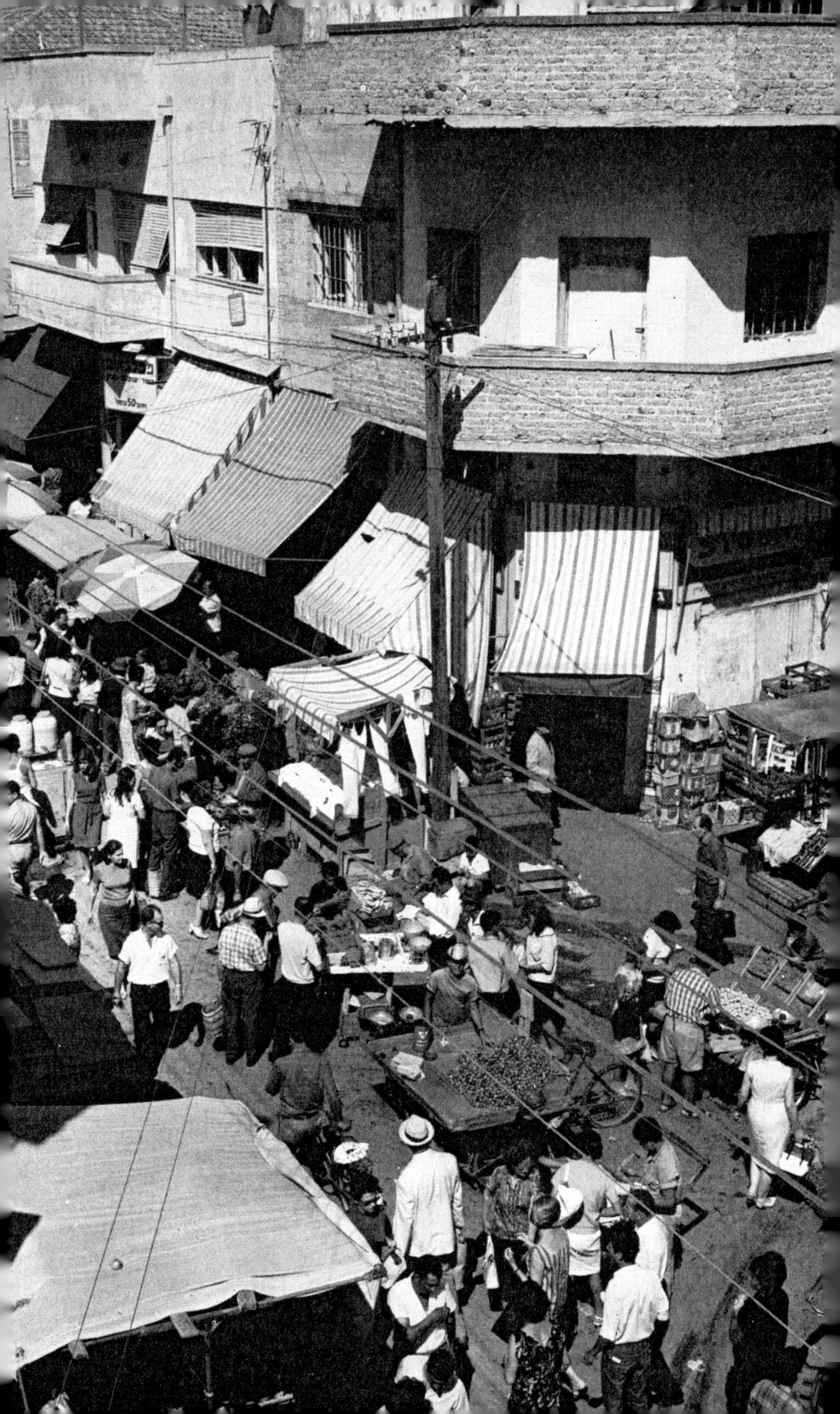

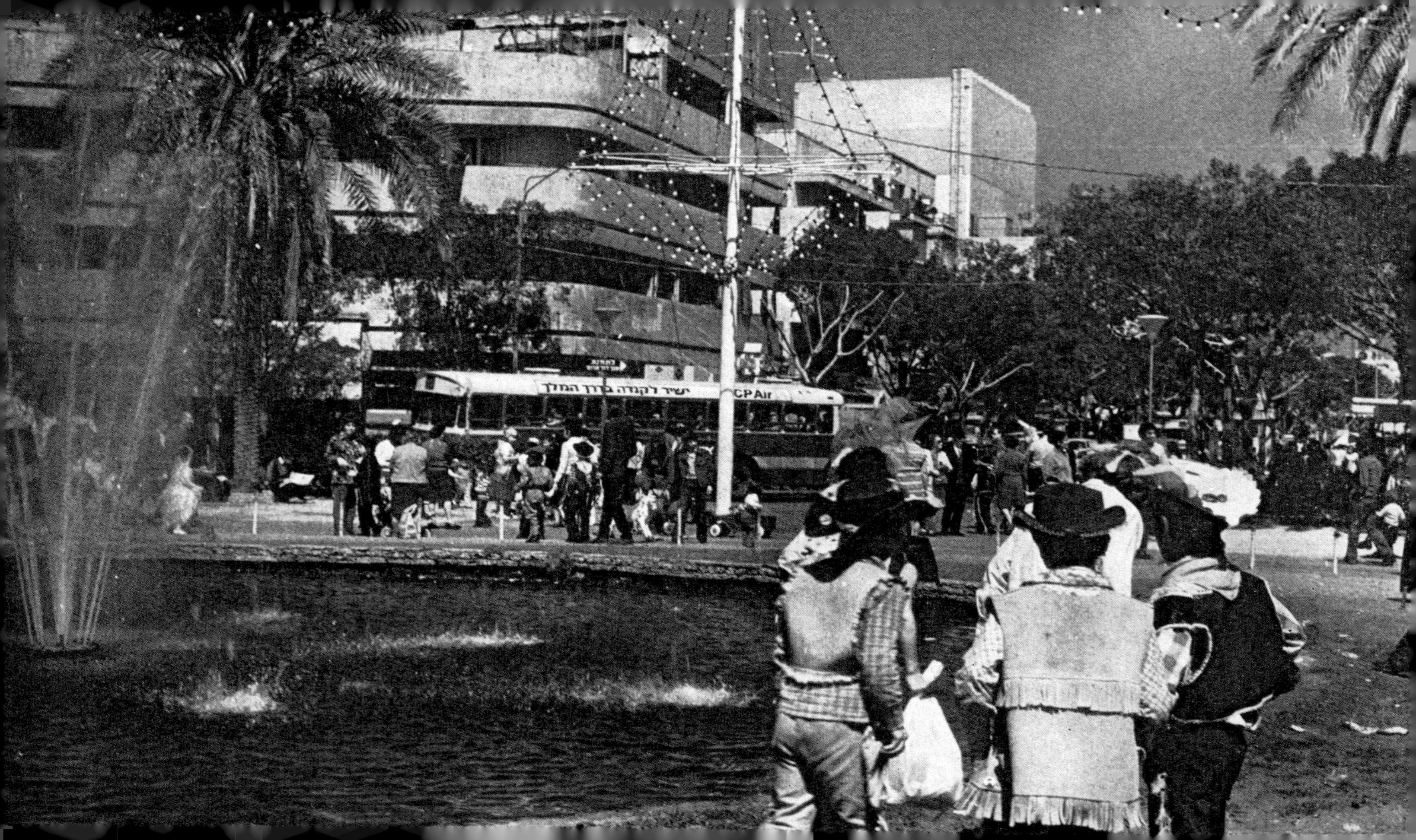
ישיר לקנדה
CP Air

humid, the flies appalling. In winter, the short heavy rains churned the ground to mud.

Yet the city grew, mainly due to successive waves of immigration. While Jaffa, as it was then known, declined, the population of Tel Aviv rose, from less than 2,000 at the end of the First World War to 165,000 at the beginning of the Second, to 350,000 by 1952. After independence, Tel Aviv-Yafo became one city, numbering 400,000 inhabitants—with Tel Aviv first in importance. A recent census showed that, while in 1948 the approximate population per square kilometer was 1834, by 1972 it had expanded by nearly three times the size to 5324! Itself begun as a suburb, Tel Aviv in turn generated new suburbs. In the first years of the 1970s, the population appeared to be declining. The answer was simple. People were moving out as Tel Aviv spread itself, the suburbs becoming towns in their own right.

To the south, there was pleasant Bat Yam ('daughter of the sea') with its own Town Hall and a beach far cleaner than Tel Aviv's. To the north-east, Ramat-Gan, translating roughly as 'garden heights', and Givatayim became attractive and cheaper residential alternatives. Still further north, those who could afford the high-rise apartments that overlook Herzlia behind and the sea before, commuted daily. It is a delightful half-hour drive each morning down the Haifa Road with the sea to your right and, after crossing the Yarkon (the muddy creek which is Tel Aviv's version of the river on which every self-respecting metropolis stands) adds immeasurably to the city's already appalling traffic problem! Because of the heat, Israelis start work at 8 am and siesta in the shade during the hottest part of the afternoon. But the cool early-morning air becomes warmer and more humid, and stops altogether at the Yarkon. By the time the crawling lines of cars have reached central Tel Aviv, you look longingly through the windows at the middle-aged bathers who make it

14 Costumes for Purim in the centre of Tel Aviv

their custom to take a morning dip in the sea near the Dan Hotel. (If you really wish to test your endurance, make the trip by bus—if possible standing!)

Yet the true Tel Avivis love the city and will live nowhere else. It is, after all, the liveliest city in Israel—not that the others are dull but, as the saying goes, 'In Haifa they work, in Jerusalem they pray, but in Tel Aviv they play'. This is only part of the truth. Tel Aviv is also the commercial and industrial centre of the country. Nearly every big firm has its head office here and almost all the national newspapers and magazines are published in Tel Aviv. It even had a moment of glory when the State Government ruled from here for a few months before moving to the capital, Jerusalem.

Socially, it's an open city, easy to make friends in. Once you are acquainted you are invited—for drinks or coffee or a meal. Sometimes the invitation will be to a restaurant but Israelis are a home-loving people and delight in entertaining guests under their own roof. There is also an excellent scheme whereby newcomers, whether prospective immigrants, 'tudat olim'—temporary residents—or just plain tourists, can spend an evening with an Israeli family. A number of Israelis take part in the scheme and it is possible to choose a host of similar profession or interests. As well as spending a pleasant evening, it is an excellent way of getting to know how the ordinary Israeli lives and of delving a little way under the surface which is, regrettably, all that many tourists see.

One may visit the home of a not very well-paid office worker and find one wall of the tiny flat given over to a superb library of books in half-a-dozen languages. The owner of a small art-gallery (Tel Aviv abounds in them) may proudly show archaeological treasures, literally beyond value. Someone else may be a an early settler, happy to have a captive audience and at the very least, the cooking will usually be good, and much better than the average Tel Aviv restaurants which come off badly by comparison with those in Yafo where, in general, the standards are higher and the prices lower.

Tel Aviv has often been called an ugly city and compared to its detriment with Jerusalem or Haifa. At one time, this was fair comment. The optimistic suburb of Yafo developed too quickly to attend to the niceties of city planning and fine architecture—became a city, in fact, almost before it realized what was happening. In the early 50s, a wave of planning started, given impetus by Tel Aviv's growing self-recognition. It came none too soon, although continuous building and rebuilding had been going on since the sand-dunes era. But now the city's face was not merely changing, it was changing into a very attractive one. Sleazy areas there were, certainly—notably in the indeterminate southern districts between Tel Aviv and Yafo proper, with a densely-crowded and relatively poor population and a high proportion of factories—which needed, and still need, attention. But for two decades, under both right- and left-wing mayors, the civic authorities built well. The municipal architecture is clean-lined and functional with a keen appreciation of aesthetic quality, while the larger projects that are now city landmarks reflect, as they helped to establish, Tel Aviv's importance as a centre of commerce and of culture.

The spacious complex that houses the Mann Auditorium, the Helena Rubinstein Art Museum and the Habimah Theatre, was one such project. The broad plaza that accommodates it joins two fine boulevards—Chen and Rothschild—and puts a full-stop to the tail end of Dizengoff.

First of the three to be built was the concert-hall, the Frederick R. Mann Auditorium. It is the home of what is probably the world's most massively over-subscribed orchestra, the Israel Philharmonic which enjoys the proprietary interest and pride that Israelis extend to all their national institutions. The great ones of music appear here—the inaugural concert for example included performers like Tortellier and Isaac Stern.

By the side of the auditorium stands the Helena Rubinstein Art Museum but the most eye-catching building of the 3-arts complex is undoubtedly the Habimah Theatre. Its façade, a great semi-cylinder of smoked glass facing Rothschild Boulevard, rises the height of the building to reveal its foyers and curving staircase. The Habimah is Israel's National Theatre, and its players face an enthusiastic, knowledgeable and highly critical audience. The idea of forming a Hebrew theatre was first mooted at the Eleventh Zionist Congress way back in 1913, at Vienna. Founded in Moscow in 1917, the Habimah finally left for Palestine in 1932, performing a wide variety of plays—Shaw, O'Casey, the Greek dramatists, Shakespeare—in addition to maintaining its distinctively Hebrew repertoire of plays based on Jewish cultural themes, drawn from both the Diaspora and the Palestinian experience of the early settlers, and Biblical incidents (a major source of ideas).

While the Habimah has now attained the status of an international company, the Kameri is Tel Aviv's own. Founded during the Mandate in 1944, it gave shows to the troops at the front during the War of Independence and is now the municipal theatre. The city also has its share of 'Little Theatres', though they are not so numerous as the pocket-sized art galleries, and the adventurous can find at least one experimental theatre group, at any given time, learning its trade in the basements of Tel Aviv.

For visitors who speak English only, it is probably easier to go and see a film instead. In Israel, English films are not dubbed but mercifully sub-titled in Hebrew and Arabic. This need not be a distraction since they tend to fade into invisibility on the screen. On the other hand, when legible, they often require only a moderate grasp of Hebrew—and can be hilarious!

No Hebrew at all is necessary though for what is probably the most famous Tel Avivi pastime. Sitting in an outdoor café, doing nothing and talking of everything, is a popular tradition both in the Middle East and in Central Europe. The Israelis, combining both, have brought it to a fine art and devoted to it extensive portions of Tel Aviv. The result is that you may drink your coffee Turkish, Greek, Arabic, espresso or instant; hot, black, cold or iced in a tall glass; with or without (according to the proprietor's origins) Viennese pastries, ice-cream or Israeli hamburgers served with salad in 'pita' bread. You may choose a café where the waiters are efficient—sometimes too much so—or where waiting for your order is half the fun and takes up much of the evening (this is also less expensive). Above all, you can indulge your café-lounging in almost any street in central Tel Aviv and watch the passing show. The most famous, of course, is on Dizengoff, a street that—like many of its habitués—is determined to be thought a character. To be fair, it does succeed if somewhat selfconsciously and its cafés are often patronized by their own distinctive clientele.

Dizengoff wants to be elegant too and succeeds in the same way, its shops becoming classier and more expensive as it nears the boisterous lively Dizengoff Circle where the whole thing breaks down and becomes a cheerfully undignified mishmash of supermarkets, ice-cream parlours, hot-dog stands and a dozen or so bus-stops.

The street itself is named after the first mayor of Tel Aviv and the circle, or 'kikar', after his wife (actually Zena, but called Dizengoff everywhere outside the guidebooks). The mayor—coincidentally his name was Meir—was the enterprising leader of the families whose settlement north of Yafo became a city. The monument to their achievement stands at what is now the intersection of Rothschild Bouevard with Nachlat Benjamin. One block away, on Herzl Street, their first tents were erected and, later, their houses built. Dizengoff gave his to the nation for a museum and it was from here that the independent State of Israel was formally declared in 1948. In this area too stood the first public building of Tel Aviv. Reflecting the traditional Jewish passion for learning, it was a high school, the famous Herzlia Gymnasia. It was overtaken by the pace of Tel Aviv's development in the early 60s and both it and the central library nearby were demolished to make room for Israel's first skyscraper.

The Shalom Tower is the tallest building in the Middle East and you can see most of Israel from the top (where a superb mosaic floor depicting the history of the city decorates the lounge of the Tower Hotel). The Tower's local nickname is the Kolbo Shalom, translating roughly as, 'you can buy everything in the Shalom' which is true—you can. The ground floor includes a large and attractive store, a convenient post office and a supermarket. This latter is a popular outing with ulpan teachers giving cram-course Hebrew lessons to new immigrants, who herd their flock towards the irresistible delicatessen counters, thus ensuring that would-be immigrants not only learn the Hebrew for such delicacies as herring in sour cream, but are seduced into buying some as well. Halfway up the Tower, the Israel Export Institute encourages a more sophisticated commerce, displaying Israeli crafts—jewellery, prints, fashion, embroidery—for the benefit of tourists and businessmen. Although the display is, of necessity, not large, the work is of a high standard on the whole and provides a useful comparison before embarking on the hazards of a shopping spree for the more expensive souvenirs.

A stone's-throw from the Kolbo, like its poorer relative, the Souk HaCarmel, Carmel Market, packs itself into half-a-dozen streets of central Tel Aviv. The near end meets Allenby just before it runs into the sea, while the far end straggles off untidily behind the Tower. It is a concentrated, oriental version of a street market, more crowded, more varied and a good deal noisier. Dense and dazzling, it is a relatively inexpensive shopping area, its pavements a mere catwalk between the open-fronted permanent stores and the tightly packed stalls that line the roadway on both sides. (A space of about eight inches between each stall is the only escape route from pedestrian traffic jams.) Small kiosks sell falafel in pita. The smell is enticing (falafel is a concoction of ground chickpeas, fried as dumplings) but it's better avoided. The other common snack, humus and tehina served on little plates and garnished with an olive or two, is much safer, and the kebab is excellent—this especially in the Kerem Hatemanim, the Yemenite Quarier just north of the market proper.

Allenby itself is an underrated street. Broad and busy, it is one of the four main north-south arteries of the city, and suffers by comparison with the other three, (Ben Yehuda with its high-priced fashions and the futuristic fire-escape of the El Al building, Ibn Gvirol with the Irya, and Dizengoff). Nevertheless, it has one of the best bookshops in the city and a main branch of Ata for home-grown Israeli fashions; and the presence of Mograbi (Israel's equivalent of Piccadilly Circus) at one end and the Great Synagogue at the other, adds to its importance. Originally, Mograbi Square was named after the date of the Balfour Declaration—significant enough by anybody's reckoning—but the Tel Aviv temperament asserted itself and called the square after the extremely scruffy Mograbi cinema on its north side. The Great Synagogue, by contrast, is one of the most attractively graceful buildings in the whole city centre though, alas, sadly misplaced. Its white and elegant arches need space to step back and admire. Instead, one of the busiest bus stops in the street stands in front, for reasons known only to the city fathers. Catering to religious, if not aesthetic, susceptibilities, traffic is diverted when the devout make their way there on Shabbat; and around the corner, bearded pious peddlars sell the necessities of ritual—phylacteries, skullcaps and prayerbooks.

A block away on Rothschild, the Haganah Museum devotes several floors to the history of Israel's Defence Force, from its enterprising and dramatic beginnings under the Mandate. The tourist 'doing' this or that city in a day is a stock joke, but a stranger arriving in Israel can find a microcosmic history of the State in its pioneers' memorial, its skyscraper development, its religion and defence, in these few city blocks of Tel Aviv.

Here, at the end of Allenby, the difference between the two halves of the city begins to make itself felt. The boundary is drawn roughly at the Petah Tikvah Road. To the south, drab factories and close-packed neighbourhoods of sleazy, bustling streets tumble towards Yafo, mainly inhabited by the poorer Eastern Jews. A humbler commercial section of the city, it yet manages to be exotic at the same time. The Tehana Merkazit, the Central Bus Station is a good example. In an extrovert city like Tel Aviv, almost any institution in general use becomes a kind of hub of the city's social life, with its own special atmosphere and the Bus Station is no exception, being one of the liveliest spots in Tel Aviv. It's good for meeting your date, eating ice cream, catching a sherut (taxi) to Jerusalem; for buying mildly 'dirty' magazines (Israelis aren't repressed enough to be really porn-minded!), cheap fruit, kosher chopped liver, splendid patisserie and bargain-price clothes. Soldiers spend their miniscule allowance on cheap sandals, and kibbutzniks get a discount. The stalls are busily patronized, and candy-sellers peddle stickjaw toffee to the bus queues. Amid this welter of activity, the buses seem almost an afterthought—until they arrive, when the waiting queues suddenly break down into their component parts, and shopping-bags and plastic briefcases are used like lethal weapons as each Tel Avivi asserts his inalienable right to board the bus before his fellow passenger. (This applies mainly to the local bus lines. The long-distance buses provide excellent means of travelling the 38 miles to Jerusalem or the nearly 60 miles to Haifa and are, in fact, an essential method of transport—cheaper than sheruts, the 7-passenger public taxis which are themselves quite inexpensive, and quicker than most of the trains!)

But cheap and cheerful south Tel Aviv is still the comparatively less-privileged part of the city. The wealthier and less-crowded residential districts, generous with trees and gardens, the prestige architecture, the leisurely boulevards and wide modern avenues, all belong to the better-off northern half of the city—Chen, Rothschild, Nordau, Keren Kayemet (whose ultra-expensive apartments have the added attraction of Tel Aviv's mini-zoo); the newly-built residential Kikar Medina; Ibn Gvirol, classed (not altogether accurately) as one of the 'ritzier' streets of the city, with the Kings of Israel Square; and, running from Ibn Gvirol to the east, Sderot Shaul, King Saul Boulevard, containing some of the city's most important municipal buildings.

The spanking new Tel Aviv Museum stands here, covering several acres. Originating in the house and collection of the enterprising Dizengoff, the Museum was later planned to be part of the Habimah arts complex. Its site had to be changed when outraged Tel Avivis refused to allow the destruction of a cluster of ancient sycamores, where camels were brought to water in the 'old days'. The sycamores remained, the museum was moved to King Saul where it was officially opened in 1971, not far from the new Law Courts, older than the museum by a mere five years. The Museum's design was the work of two Israeli architects, Dan Eytan and Yitzchak Yasher. The four large exhibition galleries they incorporated into the building seem so comfortably unobtrusive, it is almost like viewing in a friend's oversized living-room (although it also contains a lecture hall and auditorium seating over 500).

The city's other major museum is on the northern fringes of Tel Aviv (or, according to choice, the southern fringes of Ramat Aviv) comfortably situated near the eucalyptus-lined banks of the Yarkon. The Ha-aretz, the Museum of the Land, house a number of buildings. The dome of the Lasky Planetarium is a landmark on the Haifa road, and there is a glass museum, a numismatic museum (both containing exhibits dating from the Bronze Age and a Museum of Ethnology and Folklore. This last stands at the entrance of Tel Quasile, an ancient mound or 'tel', excavated in the 1950s to reveal finds dating back to Philistine times.

A young town has sprouted here—Ramat Aviv, translating roughly as 'spring heights' (although its ground is still raw from the bulldozers), dominated by the massive campus of the Tel Aviv University. One of the newer satellite suburbs, Ramat Aviv—like Ramat Gan, its southern neighbour, Herzlia and Bat Yam—is a town in its own right but it was Tel Aviv that provided the impetus for their development and, very often, the jobs to which their inhabitants still come each day. They are now considered as part of the Greater Tel Aviv area and population figures proudly give their combined, as well as their individual totals—700,000 at the last census.

The University was the result equally of expansion and the

Israeli passion for education. Founded as the municipal university in 1956, its new campus was inaugurated in Ramat Aviv only seven years later. Today, its academic staff alone numbers nearly 2,000 and 9,000 students attend its faculties and research institutes. One might think this would be sufficient even for a city as progress-conscious as Tel Aviv. In fact, a second university, the Bar Ilan, flourishes in Ramat Gan. Founded in the devout orthodox neighbourhood of Bnei Brak a year before its secular counterpart, Bar Ilan provides excellent standards of scholarship against a background of Jewish observance. Its present size is about half that of Tel Aviv University and it has established branches in the south (Ashkelon), north (Safad) and east (Tzemach, in the Jordan Valley).

But Tel Aviv's biggest development plans are for its seashore; a seashore that, in a few years time, may be invisible to all but the residents of its most modern hotels, the decorative giants springing up the length of the coast all the way to Jaffa. Tel Aviv takes its tourists seriously, and with good reason. Tourism is a rapidly expanding industry and a major source of income—(the figure was 800,000 in 1972 and was hoped to reach the million mark in 1974 before the intervention of the October War). Tel Aviv is an important city in this respect because it frequently serves as the base from which travellers visit the rest of the country, and for those tourists whose trip means the road from airport to hotel, with a side trip to Jerusalem thrown in, Tel Aviv needs more than the Mediterranean beach (which is cleaner in Bat Yam or Herzlia anyway). So the best architects are called in. Yakov Rechter, for example, built the Tel Aviv Hilton, with its 16 floors towering over the beach and a small pleasant park on Hayarkon St. Its décor is splendid with copperwork, delighting the diners in King Solomon's Gourmet Restaurant or the Milk and Honey Bar. In vigorous competition with the Hilton's seafront swimming-pool and concrete tennis courts, the Sheraton has saunas and a lobby decorated with a vast chunk of native stone while the Dan has Tiffany's Discothèque standing opposite the only 'English Pub' in Israel—a meeting place for trendy Tel Aviv. Less frivolous tastes are also catered for—one hotel, the Deborah, even has a synagogue, and two restaurants (lest meat and milk be mixed contrary to dietary law); and future standards may be sampled in advance at the Tadmore, a training hotel set in the quiet environs of Herzlia. The Government's investments and tax concessions are amply repaid by an industry that has started to bring the country around $200 million in hard currency.

Yafo, or Jaffa, is now the 'old town'—a faithful description even if Tel Aviv had never existed. It was old in Solomon's time, the harbour of Joppa to which King Hiram of Tyre shipped his cedars from Lebanon to be taken up to Jerusalem for the building of the Temple. Five hundred years earlier, in the fifteenth century BC it was mentioned as a conquest of Thothmes III. For centuries it was Jerusalem's natural outlet to the sea and was destroyed with the city when Jerusalem fell in its last desperate revolt against the Romans. Its very antiquity seems to have gathered legends around it.

It was from Joppa that Jonah took ship for Tarshish before being swallowed by the whale that spat him up again by Ashkelon, and a rock in its harbour is as firmly chained to the Greek legend of Andromeda as ever she was chained to the rock, to be rescued by Perseus; and another maiden was saved when that later hero, St George, slew the dragon here.

Over the centuries, in the constant tug-of-war between the great empires of the ancient world, Jaffa suffered the fate of the rest of Palestine and was many times destroyed and rebuilt. Egypt, Greece and Rome conquered it. The Crusaders used it as a seaport and pilgrims landed here on their way to Jerusalem. The Turks ruled it until modern times and Napoleon's army ravaged it in the eighteenth century. A more recent destruction lies at the door of the British, who dynamited a section of the city during a period of Arab rioting in the 1930s. By the time of Independence, the much-battered port was a huddle of dismal streets, mean little houses and general squalor. It was ripe for the redevelopment schemes that, a few years later, were taking hold of Tel Aviv and beautifying that city and in 1960 the Jaffa Development Corporation was founded and went to work.

Its most picturesque achievement is, beyond a doubt, the restoration of the old quarter that climbs the hillside at the sea's edge to overlook the port. The hill is really a mound, or 'tel', and is the site of the ancient town, though the houses of the restored quarter go back no further than the last century, when they were built under the Turkish administration, and the earliest mosque dates from the eighteenth century. The restoration was carried out with a sensitive regard for the character of the old district, aiming less at rigidly exact reproduction than at a harmonious re-creation of atmosphere and style. With a crowning touch of imagination, the place was settled as an artists' quarter and a flourishing colony of painters and craftsmen now live and work here.

Approached from the southern side, the rock-tinted walls (often cunningly pigmented to hide patching cement) with their tiny arched windows look like cave-dwellings for sophisticated troglodytes. Lower down the street, a broad shallow flight of steps serves the dual purpose of climbing the hill and halting the cars gently but firmly at the bottom. Inside the quarter, a dozen close-walled alleys trap time peacefully. Named after the signs of the zodiac, each turning has its little plaque of glazed ceramic (mazal dagim, for instance, is 'lucky fish'—Pisces). Open doorways lead off to the cool recesses of studios and galleries and, on the far side, narrow stone stairways lead irresistibly down towards the sea. An eighteenth-century mosque stands here, called Boutrous (Peter), on the site of Simon the Tanner's house, where St Peter brought Tabitha back to life, according to Christian tradition. A monastery and church dedicated to the apostle stand on the crest of the hill, the monastery rising on the foundations of a Crusader citadel built in the thirteenth century. An Armenian church stands broodingly next-door, overlooking the broad piazza called the Square of the Ancients because of its walled-off excavations of Jaffa's ancient history.

The esplanade leads down from the rareified heights of the artists' quarter to the town square which is the hub of Yafo, passing on the way the excellent Museum of Antiquities. The settlement of Jaffa dates, after all, from the Stone Age and the whole area is rich in archaeological finds. The Museum contains, among other things, a reconstructed model of the ancient city and itself stands among excavations. Once past here, 'present-day' Yafo starts—noisy, dirty and volatile. The harbour is still in use (though it declined in importance with the development of Haifa and Tel Aviv) and at night the fishermen sail out to net the sardine catch. The town square is a cheerful confusion of colour and sound. There is a busy police station and a constant traffic jam. There is a clock-tower built in 1917 by a Turkish Sultan, Abdul Hamid, with later additions by kibbutznikim from Ashdod Yakov, their stained glass windows telling Jaffa's history. There are the inevitable street stalls, stacked with melons big as beach-balls and weighing about 5 lbs. The restaurants are Eastern, open-fronted to the street. For a few lirot you can buy the best lunch in the city—lamb, sliced sizzling from the spit and tucked neatly into salad-stuffed pita bread. Cautious tourists watch you eating, visibly wondering whether it's 'safe' (it is) and, if you are a regular customer, the owner will correct your ungrammatical Hebrew and ask when you intend to settle here.

To the right of the square, where the road begins to climb again, the minaret of the Mamoudiyeh Mosque rises serenely above the polyglot activity. To the left, the road leads to the even busier Flea Market—its appealing Hebrew translation is Shouk Hapishpishim. The market is famous, and completely different in character from the Carmel in Tel Aviv. No food is sold in its narrow arcades. Instead, the antique (or the merely second-hand) is displayed in a profusion of brassware, silver and jewelled ornaments. Among the plastic trinketry and junk, there is enough of genuine value for the whole market to be sealed off with iron shutters when the stalls close for the night and the traders go home.

Beyond the town centre, the road straggles uphill through an undistinguished cluster of small factories and warehouses to the immigrants' club and ulpan at the top of the rise. (A kind of *alma mater* for many new arrivals, the cram courses in instant Hebrew are rendered pleasant by the view over the sea from its classroom windows). The street, Rehov Yefet, looks unpromising enough but a little further on, a side street tilts down toward the harbour and enters a different world, of Arab houses and sun-bleached peeling walls. It has an obscurely sinister reputation and its casually untidy streets are different again from the calculated elegance of the artists' quarter. It is, in a word, authentic, giving a vivid glimpse of the Arab waterfront town of Turkish times, before the road continues south and Yafo gives way to Bat Yam.

8. The Negev

Where does the Negev begin? The question is often asked by puzzled tourists, particularly those coming from the north where the Judean Wilderness gives way to the Negev almost imperceptibly. A line drawn roughly from the lower tip of the Dead Sea, tilting slightly to take in the town of Arad and thence reaching towards the Gaza Strip, provides probably the most accurate answer. The word 'negev', in fact, means south, and the area continues as far as Eilat and across to Sinai. It formed part of the ancient trade routes and there is evidence that, in the past, the ports on the Gulf of Suez—Abu Rodeis and Abu Zeneima—served as starting points for the caravans. They loaded their merchandise, brought by ship from as far away as Ethiopia, to be transported north and east across Sinai and the Negev to the rich markets of Damascus and Baghdad. Today the emphasis has shifted slightly. Mountainous to the south, its northern half is Israel's very own prairie and the Negev is the prime example of the country's attempts to 'make the desert bloom'.

Much has been done over the years to develop the desert's agricultural potential. The importance of this effort is understandable when it is realized that the Negev comprises two-thirds of Israel's total land area.

A journey through the Negev is little short of spellbinding: its ever-changing colours shimmer in the heat haze and rock formations baked by the sun seem bizarre. Here and there, the farming settlements show a brave green and even manage to water their tiny gardens and communal lawns in the very centre of the desert. Nearer the coast, the land is more rewarding. Travelling southwest from Ashkelon, the route winds through cotton fields and vineyards and banana plantations. The fields are dotted with beehives and hothouses, and the kibbutzim are shaded by sycamore and fast-growing eucalyptus, mulberry and bohinia; and there even small, newly-planted forests.

Even so, the Negev of 1974 still falls short of the vision of Ben Gurion, one of the architects of modern Israel and its first Prime Minister—'... there will be cottages all over the country ... (no skyscrapers) ... we will have small towns, villages filled with flowers and trees and lots of children....' Yet Ben Gurion lived to see a good many of his dreams come true—25 years later, there were 1000 villages, compared with the mere 300 or so of 1948. His own kibbutz, Sde Boker, stands some 30 miles south of Beersheba, a flourishing settlement and a testimony to his vision. Nor is it the only one. The list is long—Misaf Arad, Tel Arad, Rosh Zohar, Ein Bokek, Massada, Ein Avdat, Mitzpeh Ramon, and many more; but it is sad that reality is more in harmony with Albert Camus than with Ben Gurion, for it was the former who said in 1957, '... they had to forge themselves an art of living in times of catastrophe in order to be reborn, and then fight openly against the death instinct at work in our history...'.

Beersheba, the 'capital' of the Negev, is also its major town. Traditionally the southern border of ancient Israel, Biblical Beersheba is now being excavated at a tel north of the modern city. The Negev has been traversed by man for 35 centuries and the earliest settlement at Beersheba goes back to 4,000 BC.

It derived its importance partly from its position at the crossroads of four vital routes, south and west from the Mediterranean and Egypt, north and east from Hebron and the Arava. The origins of its name are given in the book of Genesis. Beersheba

15 *The Dead Sea rift and the fortress of Massada*

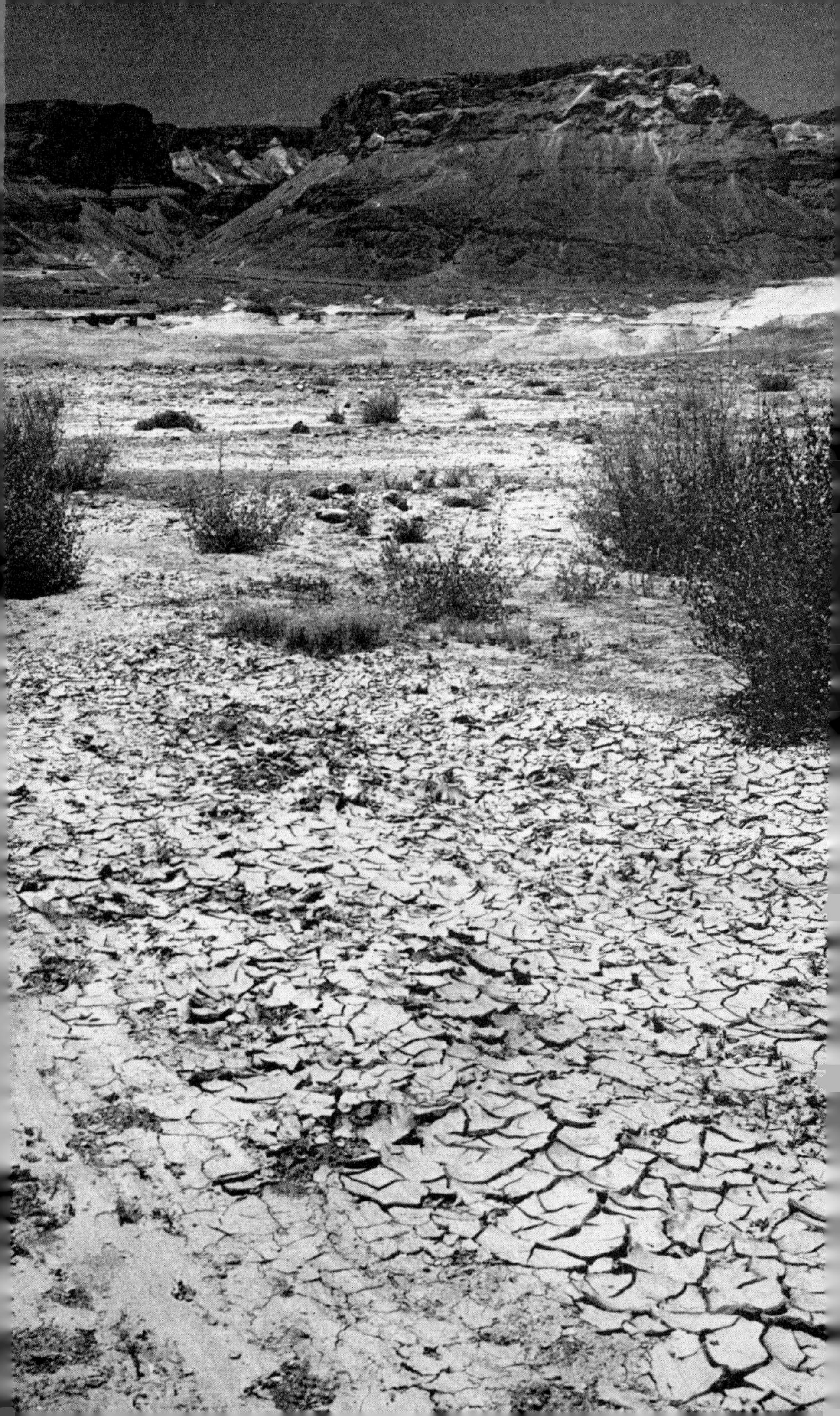

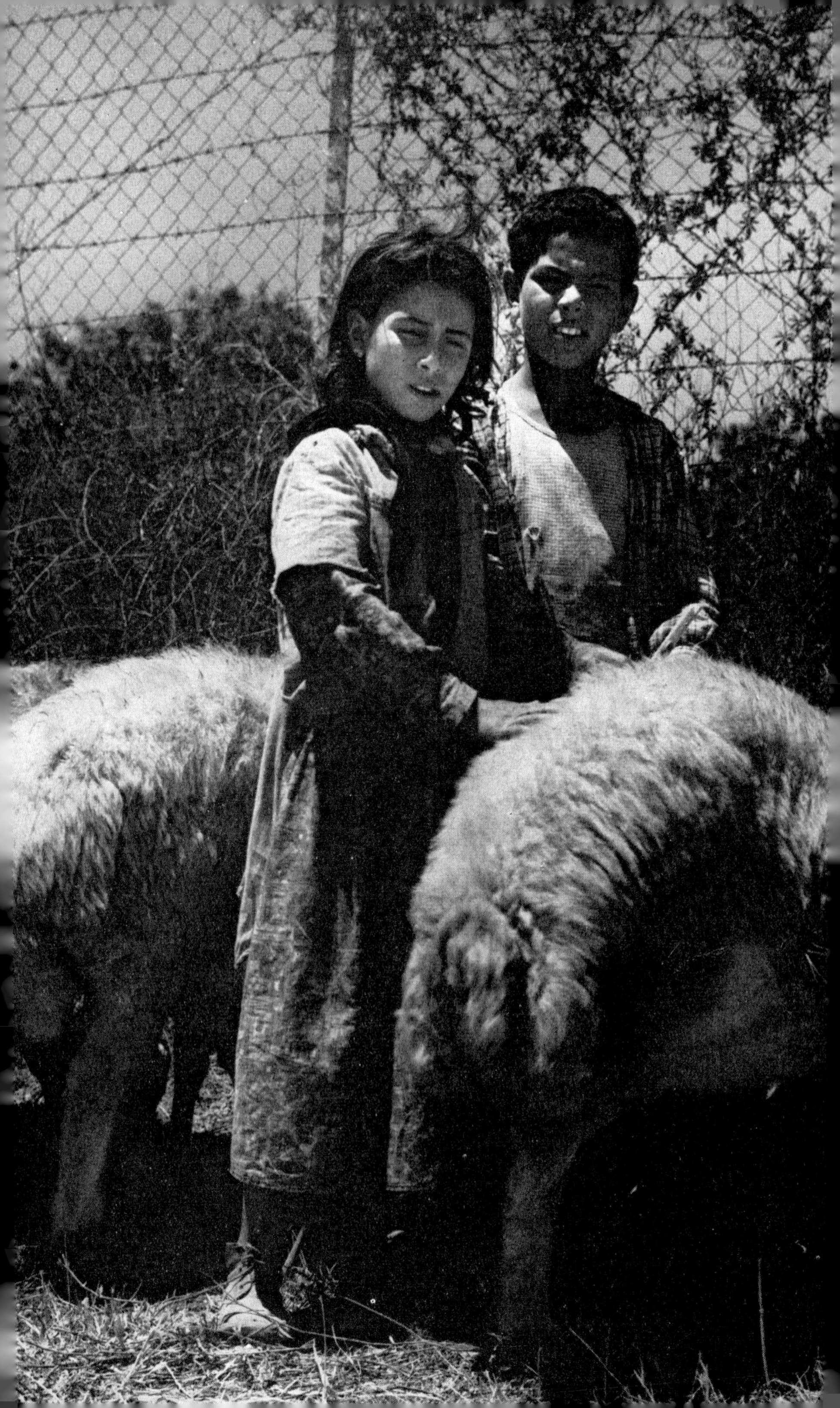

was the site where Abimelech, King of Gerar, received an oath from Abraham. *Shvah* means 'oath' in Hebrew and *beer* (as in bear) is 'well'—hence Beersheva, the 'well of the oath': 'And Abraham set seven ewe lambs of the flock by themselves ... Wherefore he called the place Beer Sheba; because there they sware both of them'.

The modern town developed with astonishing rapidity from a dreary cluster of mud houses when Israel took it over in 1948. It now boasts workers' housing and good hotels, shopping centres and restaurants and is the home of one of Israel's youngest universities, the University of the Negev. This remarkable institute was founded in 1965 and its three faculties—Humanities and Social Sciences, Engineering, and Natural Sciences—are under the academic supervision of the Hebrew University, the Haifa Technion or the Weizmann Institute. A staff of about 550 teach some 2,000 students and the first degrees were awarded in 1969. The hub of the town is the old Turkish mosque and, as the city expands, some of the most advanced experiments in desert housing are being carried out by Israel's architects.

Nor is culture lacking. Beersheba, with its population grown to 100,000 (from less than 20,000 a decade ago) serves as a cultural centre and together with the inhabitants of the townships and settlements round about, makes heavy demands on the country's orchestras and theatre groups. But the main object, of course, is development and the aim of the Arid Zone Research Centre, housed in Beersheba, is to make the desert habitable and to encourage industrial expansion in the Negev. An area of land has already been selected for an industrial complex which will be directed and operated by local and central government bodies and the University.

Despite its air of progress, Beersheba is unchanged in one respect, at least. The Bedouin still come in from the surrounding

16 Bedouin children with fat-tailed sheep

J

desert to use the town, as they have for centuries, as a marketplace and as a trading centre. Their stalls can be seen on any day of the week but their traditionally famous market is still held on Thursdays, in the early hours of the morning. The new and impressive municipal market just across the way is no match for the dirty and colourful Bedouin bazaars, exotic with skins and spices—though these are displayed impartially (and regrettably), alongside cheap shoes, plastic table ware and .tourist souvenirs!.

The Bedouin are an amalgam of contradictions, in fact, about whom romantic Western visitors cherish inaccurate visions of desert warriors and regal chieftains. The reality of the Bedouin mode of life is one of ignorance and hardship, poverty and endemic disease—notably tuberculosis and eye and skin ailments. Over 20,000 Bedouin, members of 18 tribes, live in the Beersheba and Shoval regions of the northern Negev—the largest concentration in the country. A good many have opted for a more sedentary mode of life and the sight of a Bedouin driving a car or a tractor, living in a house instead of a tent, and dressed in Western style, is no longer unusual although the majority still live in the old way—raising sheep and camels, living in impermanent sprawling encampments in black goat-hair tents among the neighbouring kibbutzim.

Increasing exposure to the standards of an industrial society is gradually doing away with much of the hardship of the Bedouin way of life. But progress has its other side. As long as the tribal life continues, its direction can be controlled by the tribe for land and possessions are familial, not personal. The new ways and the increased disenchantment with the tribal system have weakened the family ties and, as the social structure loosens, more and more Bedouin make the confusing transition from tribesman to individual.

For the Bedouin, the change is most noticeable in the economic sphere. He is now a consumer. An open fire for cooking is now a rare sight, plastics have replaced copper and the transistor radio is more in evidence than the traditional reed pipe. One custom, however, remains unchanged—that of bride-purchase; and in these inflationary times, it is a major factor prodding the young men of the tribe to improve their financial status—which, paradoxically, they can only do by breaking with their traditional occupations and entering the twentieth-century way of life. It will be a long time before the process is fully complete and, for the present, the Bedouin are still one of the most colourful and highly individual peoples, wandering in and out of Israel's modern life as they choose.

To the east, the Negev stretches to the Dead Sea. A fast new road hugs the coastline passing Massada and Ein Bokek on the way to Sodom. From there, it runs straight as an arrow through the unrelieved desert landscape southwards to Yotvata, to Solomon's Pillars and nearby Timna and thence to Eilat.

Until recently, a pilgrimage to Massada was a feat of considerable endurance. That was before the cable-car was built but, even now, many visitors still prefer the arduous climb. Homage to the memory of those who fell at Massada, they contend, is not just a matter of standing respectfully on the flat-topped forbidding mountain. The difficulties of the ascent allow time for reflection on the fate of the few who, in AD 73 committed mass suicide rather than surrender to the Romans.

The climb is exciting in itself, but it also symbolizes the belief that tyranny in any form is evil, to come to terms with it is to surrender—and that surrender means slavery. The modern Israeli is being quite specific when he says 'Massada shall not fall again'. The world is full of Massadas and wherever the example of those on the mountain is emulated, the same battle is joined.

Historian Josephus' account of Massada is superlative drama, and the discoveries of recent years have testified to the truth of his account. According to Josephus, the fortress was first built during the reign of the Hasmonean High Priest, Yochanan. The main fortifications and the luxurious palace were added by Herod who chose Massada as the perfect stronghold, a place of refuge from the popular uprising he constantly feared. Massada's greatest hour came almost a century later. By AD 70, Jerusalem had been raised and the Temple destroyed. Emperor Titus believed that the Jewish rebellion had been crushed—as, indeed, it had been except for the small band of Zealots numbering about a thousand or so who had decided on a determined stand against the might of the Empire. For the next three years, two men faced one another—Silva, the Roman Commander, and Eliezer ben Yair, the Zealot—one for the honour of Rome, the other for the love of freedom. The fortress remained impregnable for three years until finally Silva built a gigantic ramp which enabled him to reach the walls of the fortress and set fire to them. Watching the flames on that fateful day, the Zealots knew their time had come. Yair ordered the destruction of all possessions except food so that 'the enemy shall see that we voluntarily chose to die rather than to submit to slavery'. Josephus goes on to recount the method by which the Zealots elected to die. Ten men were chosen by lot to put the voluntary martyrs to the sword. Then one of the ten was chosen, also by lot, to end the lives of his nine companions. The remaining defender set fire to the palace and impaled himself on his sword.

The defenders' heroism was transcribed for posterity by Josephus from the account of the few women and children remaining alive after the three-year siege.

At the foot of the mountain, the great plain reflects brightly in the sunlight. Covered in a soft layer of dust, it creates the illusion of fantastic towers, walls and fortresses; but seen from this angle, there is no illusion about the mountain, which looms square and forbidding above the while soil of the plain around it.

The search for lost cities holds tremendous fascination—so, too, the heap of salt which is all that is left of ancient Sodom. It forms convoluted stony shapes—any one of which could resemble the outlines of Lot's wife, who dared to look back upon the destruction of Sodom and Gomorrah, 'the cities of the plain', and paid the penalty by being turned into a pillar of salt. As one writer puts it, if she looked back now, all she would see is the Dead Sea Potash Plant, the main centre of activity in the area, moved from

The Negev 149

the northern end of the Dead Sea after the war of 1948.

The approach to Sodom, or Sdom as it is called, is weirdly surrealistic. The sky appears to close in, the earth seems deserted and everything upon it is motionless. The cause of all this is, prosaically enough, the potash works, its tall smoke stacks and white powdery haze creating the optical illusion through which, a few moments later, modern Sdom emerges to dispel the atmosphere of the old story of the tragedy and of the Divine wrath that consigned Sodom and Gomorrah to perpetual oblivion. Whatever the myth and its attractions, one must ruefully accept the facts of plausible scientific explanations for the cataclysm that blew up this section of the earth.

The administrative centre of the area is Neve Zohar, where the amenities include a guest house, a camp site and youth hostel; and, typically Israeli, there is also a museum, devoted to the Dead Sea region. The bleak and desolate landscape is relieved by the nearby (and sole) sweet-water spring of Ein Bokek. But a little further south of the potash works, a turn-off along a dirt road leads to Ne'ot Hakikar where there are half-a-dozen small springs, most of them brackish, where the vegetation has adapted to the conditions. The settlers here, all youngsters, grow dates and raise cattle and supplement their income with a sideline (again typically Israeli)—organized desert tours in heavy-duty command cars. This has proved the only really effective way of exploring the Negev. The vehicles are capable of tackling the deep ravines and winding canyons that would otherwise be impassable. They can negotiate rocky defiles to reach the plateaux that afford breathtaking views of the Dead Sea.

Nothing swims, or lives beneath the glazed surface of the Dead Sea. Nothing can sink in it, either—with about half a pound of salt per quart it has eight times the concentration found in ordinary seawater. Salt marshes separated by dikes cover the area around the Sea almost to the very edges of the shoreline. When the water evaporates, the heavy crystalline layers of salt emerge, flashing and sparkling in the sunlight. And again an odd note of surrealism creeps in. A man in a bathing suit ambles nonchalantly into the water, settles comfortably and proceeds to read a newspaper; presently, another joins him—with a tray of drinks! Soon, cushioned by the buoyancy of the heavily salted water, both relax with papers that need not get wet and a tray of drinks they need not hold.

Much mystery, however, still surrounds the Sea. There is, for example, speculation about the cause of the peninsula that narrows the strait between Jordan and Israel to about five miles, at the Sea's southern tip, and the peninsula is the subject of considerable study and research. Geologists think it quite probably that the Lashon—the tongue—as the peninsula is called in Hebrew, is not an integral part of the Dead Sea; and that it could have come about as a result of one of the fairly frequent earthquakes in ancient times. This theory is given much support by the tale of Sodom and Gomorrah, and the search on the Sea's bed for the remnants of the destroyed cities continues unabated.

Industry is here, too. A potassium plant processes the valuable mineral, extracting the thousands of tons needed to fill domestic and export requirements, potassium being one of Israel's main earners of foreign exchange. The Dead Sea's pungent brine contains incredibly high amounts of bromine—a major reason for Israel's dramatically swift expansion of the chemical and pharmaceutical industries (bromine has further uses in petrol processing and in agriculture). It is in this context that the Bible plays the modern secular role of guide, indicating where the next prospecting may be profitably carried out—a valuable source of practical geological information.

On the way to Eilat, to Timna and the fabled King Solomon's Mines, one further stop is of interest. This is the settlement of Yotvata founded, as far as one can tell, for two reasons. The first is almost *de rigeur* in Israel—it was settled in Biblical days, being mentioned in the books of Numbers and of Deuteronomy. The second reason—and the one given by its young founders—is that they were tired of their parents' incessant boasting about their own pioneering achievements! So, from various parts of Israel, the settlers have come to prove the point that there is still sufficient mettle in the country's youth to lure them away from more lucrative occupations in the towns to become hard-working, self-made farmers. The farmers of Yotvata supply Eilat with a whole range of produce. Their trucks also make daily journeys to supply the markets of the north with their excellent dairy produce and greens; and from having once been merely a halt along the journey across the desert from Egypt to Canaan, Yotvata now offers a welcome respite from the desert.

The greatest development of the Eilat region took place under Solomon, and he is credited with having developed the copper mines named after him at Timna. Solomon's Pillars loom magnificently some distance from the mining areas, bizarre formations in beautiful rose-coloured rock. The Timna mines are still an integral part of Eilat's economy and that of the surrounding area. At any given time, they provide employment for between 400 and 600 families in the locality.

To transport his copper, Solomon built up his fleets of merchant shipping. 'And King Solomon made a navy of ships in Etzion Geber, which is beside Elath, on the shore of the Red Sea, in the land of Edom ... and they came to Ophir ...' (Kings 1, 9). Etzion Geber was thought by some to have been the site of the mines in fact, and the question is still being debated. Excavations carried out by the late Professor Glueck of Cincinatti unearthed remnants of a fort dating back to Israelite times and smelting furnaces with remains of copper and waste.

Solomon's ships sailed from Eilat and the port was the commercial base for trade with Africa and Asia. Although it was the town's most prosperous period, its importance had been long established. It was mentioned in Deuteronomy as a station along the route taken by the Children of Israel to the Promised Land and achieved economic prominence when the powerful kingdoms that ruled in the Negev and Edom developed the trade routes and began the exploitation of natural resources.

Israelites had settled in the area since the reign of David and Eilatis are very proud of the fact that here Solomon welcomed the Queen of Sheba. Following his death, the commercial life of the region declined until the establishment of the Nabatean kingdom caused it to revive. Centuries later, it fell to the Muslim conquest and later still, the Crusaders, recognizing Eilat's value, captured it in 1124.

Eilat has been variously described as the Gateway to the East; as the threshold of Asia and Africa; as the end of the world; as a kind of service entrance. Approaching it, one glimpses first the sister town of Akaba reflected in the clear Gulf waters. A moment later, the traveller is driving by the full length of Eilat's airport and into the town itself.

When Palestine was partitioned by the decision of the United Nations in 1947 the Negev, which was allocated to the Jewish State, included a part of the narrow strip of coastline at the northern tip of the Gulf of Eilat (or Akaba, as it was officially designated). The little village of Akaba on the eastern side became part of the kingdom of Jordan while the part given to Israel comprised a dismal police outpost known as Um Rashrash and precious little else. Not until 10 months after Independence was declared did the Israelis physically occupy the area. Then foundations for the new town were dug all around the police post and work began in earnest.

From such modest beginnings, Eilat has grown to a population exceeding 15,000 and is still expanding. As a tourist attraction, it ranks high, drawing great numbers of visitors throughout the year including underwater fishing enthusiasts and would-be explorers of the surrounding desert. Other visitors simply come because the weather is good and the waters are pure pleasure, even in December.

Eilat's improvement projects seek to fulfil its aquatic destiny and become the 'Venice of the Red Sea'. The multi-million dollar programme is designed to make Eilat the best equipped seaside resort in the Middle East, with unique features. Already in evidence are the new canals and lagoons; and it is hoped that marinas and a resort centre surrounding the main lagoon will cater for thousands of visitors by the mid-70s. Other bold ideas include floating islands for restaurants and nightclubs, and a glass-sheathed 'Aquascope' for a submarine view of Eilat's famous corals and rare tropical fish.

For the moment, one of the results of Eilat's expansion is its airport. It is being moved five miles north of the town, expanded into an international gateway with direct flights to Europe. Communications with the rest of the country are excellent and the domestic airline, Arkia, has nine to ten flights daily from Eilat to Jerusalem or Tel Aviv. There are also daily coach services and the railway line from Beersheba to Dimona will eventually be extended south to Eilat.

Of the many excursions into the surrounding country, one of the most interesting for those hardy enough to take it, is a day in the Eilat mountains. The 12-seater jeeps used for the tour travel along the Coral Bay towards Emek Shlomo—a trail famous for over 1,000 years as the caravan route for the perfumes of Arabia, between the Red Sea and the Mediterranean. In the Second World War when Rommel threatened Alexandria and Cairo, the British Army patched up the all-but-forgotten route for use as a possible emergency exit from the area, in the event of a successful German advance. The Emek Shlomo trail was also part of the pilgrims' road (Darb el-Haj) to Mecca. Fascination, surprise and wonder are perhaps the predominant feelings when travelling through this stark landscape of gullies, seemingly vast flat stretches and strange formations of black granite looming against the sky. At Ein Nefatim, once a border point with Egypt, the effects are even more striking. The most meagre rainfall is followed, after a few days, by a thick carpet of unexpected flowers. After a dry spell, there is the spectacle of dull and shiny surfaces interchanging rapidly to give the illusion of coruscating gems.

As mentioned earlier, the Nabateans were very active in the

southern Negev following the period of decline after Solomon's death. A vigorous people, they took their name from Nabath, the son of Ishmael, the hapless offspring of Abraham and his maidservant, Hagar. It is presumed that they originated in the Arabian desert and that the nearby Jordanian city of Petra was their capital. They were sharp traders and skilful politicians and fighters. Allied with the Hasmoneans (or Maccabeans) in their struggles against Rome, the Nabateans succeeded in retaining their identity and relative independence through 700 years of changing fortunes, until their defeat and near-extinction by the Persians in AD 416.

Somewhere around the second century BC they founded two villages near the route from Petra across to the Mediterranean—Shivta and Avdat. The 'cities' straddle the ancient caravan route through the Nahal Zin valley and their histories are more or less similar. The key to their existence was water and Avdat was in the singularly fortunate position of having its own spring—Ein Avdat. Still, the town might not have attained its undoubted prominence (its population at the time was believed to number some 6,000 souls) had it not been for Nabatean expertise in water storage and conservation. Their achievements in this field are tremendous and are still the subject of research by present-day experts. Nabatean methods are being used in experiments by modern agricultural scientists to determine their efficiency—although, for over 13 centuries, the desert covered all traces of this vanished people.

The name Avdat has its origins in that of the Nabatean king, Obodos, a contemporary of Herod. Like its sister 'city', Shivta, Avdat was taken by Trajan in AD 106 and revived again under a later emperor, Diocletian. The area flourished in Byzantine times when, as usual, a good deal of ecclesiastical building was carried on; but, with the area's later decay, Avdat stood desolate until the present century. An Israeli reconstruction team moved in to restore Avdat—mainly the Byzantine section, leaving the Roman part for later. Among the most interesting structures at the site is

The Negev

the Roman-Byzantine bath-house, rebuilt at the foot of a slope. (Nearby are more modern facilities, including a gas-station and restaurant). The source of water for the baths is an ancient well, descending 60 meters to the water table below the surface. There was also an ingenious heating system. The baths had double floors criss-crossed by pipes through which hot air was pushed by external heaters. Water was then poured over the hot surface resulting in immediate evaporation which caused the room to be filled with steam. The Byzantines subsequently improved the baths and, in addition, built St Theodore's church, one of the first in the land. It is excellently preserved, except for the roof and next-door stands a monastery, the ruins of which lead to the castle and beyond to the watch-tower. There are even traces of the Nabateans remaining—an altar, a necropolis and the water cisterns.

The Avdat plateau has several gullies which cut deeply into its near-vertical sides. One of these is Nahal Zin, where the rock wall towers nearly 100 meters above the ground. Here and there, the surface is dotted with nodules forming weird patterns and a walk along the Nahal Zin (lined with reeds through which water trickles even at the height of the dry season) leads to a natural pool at the foot of a small waterfall whose source is the tranquil spring of Ein Mor.

About five miles north, standing as if in the middle of nowhere, is the village of Sde Boker. It is, in fact, a kibbutz founded in the early 1950s by a group which included Israel's first Prime Minister, David Ben Gurion. The Sde Boker College, not far away, was named after his wife, Paula. The creation of Sde Boker was in great part due to that almost limitless audacity which the Israelis call *chutzpah*. The place was desolate and empty, without pasture or sufficient water for any but the most basic purposes, neglected and forgotten. But, in the caves of this unpromising region, there were prehistoric paintings—proving that long ago, man had lived here. That knowledge, and *chutzpah*, were all the group needed as encouragement to go ahead. Sde

Boker now is a flourishing monument to their dedicated efforts. Ben Gurion returned continually throughout his life and, as one of the leaders of the little group, may have drawn his inspiration not only from the ancient prophets of Israel, but from the best-known and greatest of his contemporaries, Winston Churchill—'The impossible takes a little longer'.

9. The Borders

The great triangle of Sinai covers around 60,000 square kilometers of desert and mountains. A bleak and desolate region where temperatures can reach a punishing 120 degrees, it has at the same time a beauty and grandeur all its own. It is a land of eroded soil and granite peaks, bizarre rock formations and the ever-changing colours of the deserts, hinting sometimes at the mineral wealth that lies beneath—turquoise for copper, red for iron, black for manganese.

Somewhat surprisingly, in view of its inhospitable terrain, Sinai has always known human presence. From immemorial times, it was crisscrossed by the trade routes that linked Africa and Asia, constantly traversed by laden caravans journeying from one end of the Fertile Crescent to the other. The roads ran along Sinai's northern edge, the coastal plain of the Mediterranean, where a belt of scrub and sand dunes is punctuated here and there by groves of date palms and a few settlements, the only town of importance being El Arish.

Another major highway runs parallel, some 30 miles south—the road from Ismailia on the Suez Canal to Nitsana just inside the Israeli border. It lies not far from the Gidi and Mitla Passes, the latter of which figured so prominently in the Sinai Campaign of 1956 and in the 6-day War, 10 years later. The Mitla is a long narrow defile on the road that forms the pilgrim route to Mecca. In 1956, the Israeli paratroopers dropped behind the enemy lines 100 miles in front of the ground forces, seized and held the Pass at heavy cost. The 1967 war again brought fierce battles to the pass when the Egyptians were cut off, mainly by Israeli airpower, and their equipment and vehicles destroyed.

The high plateau of southern Sinai is fittingly named E-Tih, 'Aimless Wanderers', a reference to the handful of nomads who live here. The peasants tend to settle along the coastal areas but there are between 30,000 and 40,000 Bedouin who maintain their age-old freedom in a desert way of life.

It is hardly necessary to turn to the Bible to recall Sinai's most dramatic links with history—the 40-year wandering of the Children of Israel in the wilderness of Sin and the Giving of the Law on Mount Sinai. 'And the Lord came down upon Mount Sinai, to the top of the mount, and the Lord called Moses to the top of the mountain; and Moses went up.' He received the Ten Commandments there and the sublime event is said to have taken place among the towering red peaks of southern Sinai. Tradition has located the mountain and called it Mount Sinai, or Jebel Musa (Moses' mountain), despite scholarly scepticism. The scholars, indeed, have long puzzled over the exact route of the Children of Israel as they were led by Moses through the wilderness and some believe it lay far north along the coastal plain. But the desert hermits accepted tradition, dwelling in the region around Jebel Musa in the early centuries AD. St Catherine's Monastery at its foot was founded in the fourth century in honour of a young Alexandrian martyr. It is a treasure-house of religious art and manuscripts and once possessed the oldest known copy of the New Testament. A custom of the monastery is to preserve the bones of its monks. They are laid out carefully and completely, watched over by a skeletal abbot in his robes.

A more rewarding view is that of sunrise, seen from the top of Sinai. It is customary to climb the mountain—though not, fortunately, nearby Mount Katherina, which towers a good thousand feet higher.

Less rugged but just as fascinating is the journey down Sinai's coast on the Gulf of Eilat to Sharm el Sheikh. The Bedouin fishing villages are now being joined by Israeli farming settlements—Nueiba, for example, by Nahal Neviyot, and Dahab by Di'zahav. One of the unlikelier crops grown is cucumbers and the Bedouin have found seasonal employment as agricultural labourers. Some of the loveliest coral in the world is found here. The beaches are pleasant, the water blue and limpid and the camping facilities already foreshadow a more sophisticated development.

At Sharm el Sheikh, a new township is springing up, called Ofira. The little island of Tiran lies peacefully across the glittering waters but the two large spiked guns that face it from the mainland are left by Israel as a reminder that the Tiran Strait, or rather the Egyptian blockade of it in 1967, led directly to the 6-Day War. Israel is taking no chances—Ofira is a civilian township but the no-entry zone at nearby Sharm leads to a military base. At the uttermost tip of Sinai, a thin strip of land juts out like a curled finger, Ras Muhamed, or Muhamed's Head, overlooking the width of the Red Sea. The beautiful corals of the Gulf grow here too—but, typically enough, there are sharks!

The nights along the Gulf are warm—and it is not only the hippies who take their sleeping-bags to the beach and lie out under the stars. But the signs of progress are few as yet, and the name of Sinai still grips the imagination most powerfully as the wilderness where the Children of Israel, brought as slaves out of Egypt, were forged into a free nation.

The Golan Heights is the name given to the ridge of land that rises over 1,000 ft on the east shore of Kinneret (Lake Galilee), stretching northwards along the course of the Jordan and forming Syria's border with Israel. Ranged around the lake, they help to make the view over Tiberias the superb panorama that it is. Further north, some of the richest agricultural land of the area belongs to the Heights but lay unused for a number of years due to the Syrian military encampments there. It was a thickly-wooded region as far back as Biblical times, (although the last forests were felled nearly a century ago), and its ancient name was

Bashan. In the reign of David, it was part of the kingdom of Israel and the Hasmonean dynasty also ruled there. Jewish settlement was populous in Roman times and remained so until the persecutions of the Byzantine Christian Empire several centuries later. The Crusaders held it as a strategic outpost of their kingdom but lost it to the Saracen. More recently, it was settled by Druze, as witness the attractive little village of Majd el Shams, surrounded by orchards on Hermon's slopes. The triple-peaked mountain towers over the borders of Lebanon, Syria and Israel and, since the 1967 war, is slowly developing into a popular if unlikely ski resort. Not far from here, one of the Jordan's tributaries, the Banias, flows through a charming setting of wooded cliffs. The Greeks dedicated the glade to Pan, calling it Paneas, the origin of the present name. There is a natural pool and the area around it is a popular site for picnics.

Gaza, on the edge of the Sinai desert, was the most important of the five cities built by the Philistines. It lay in a rich agricultural area (today the main product is citrus fruit) and was situated in a commanding position on the caravan routes that ran north to Damascus and south to Arabia and Egypt. The Bible makes constant reference to the troublesome Philistine presence on Israel's coast to the south, culminating in the tale of Samson's destruction of Dagon's temple in Gaza, which remained unrepentantly pagan until well into the fifth century.

It was, for a time, a renowned centre of philosophy and, during the Muslim period, a large Jewish and Samaritan community settled in the town. It shared in the general stagnation of Palestine under the Ottomans, who used it as a Turkish stronghold in the First World War. Its importance rose again when Egypt occupied it in 1948, and it became the capital of the Gaza 'Strip'.

The town itself is rather drab though here and there can be seen an older Arab house, pastel-coloured, dignified and charming. Some very attractive bamboo furniture is produced here and Gaza is especially noted for its light woven fabrics, the original 'gauze' derived from its name. The few sites of interest include the Great Mosque, built on the foundations of a thirteenth-century Crusader church and Samson's Tomb, of highly doubtful authenticity, near the railway station. But the refugee camps are too near perhaps for anything but a quiet, withdrawn atmosphere of guarded neutrality. Yet the drive down the coast carries few reminders. The women are modestly veiled on the beach, where huge tents flutter in the breeze. The grape vines reach almost to the road and an offer to buy a kilo or two of the harvest meets with a generous filling of sun hats with great clusters of grapes that last all the way to Khan Yunis, Rafah, and back.

Khan Yunis is a pleasant oasis city close to the tip of the fertile plain. The ruins of the khan which gives the town its name can still be seen, one of the ancient caravanserais established by the Mamelukes along the trade roads. From here, a short drive ends the trip at Rafah, directly on the Sinai border. On Rafah's outskirts, what was a large refugee camp has gradually disappeared. Its one-time inhabitants now live in the housing suburb that has replaced it, each house with its own attractive patch of garden. The daily buses are laden with commuters going to work in the Gaza Strip or in Israel, where their labour is well paid on the local kibbutzim or on further building and development projects —a hopeful sign perhaps, for the still unsettled future.

10. The Kibbutz

Probably no other institution in Israel has aroused so much controversy or so much interest as the kibbutz. Reaction to it varies from admiration and approval to criticism and downright disbelief that the sytem could ever work. It seemed scarcely credible that a group of highly individual human beings should come together, often from wildly different environments, to lead a spartan existence whose dangers and difficulties would not even be compensated for by any material gain—where, indeed, the idea of personal possessions was totally rejected.

The kibbutz is the ultimate community of modern society, a made-in-Israel product unique to the country and the time. Attempted elsewhere, it has proved non-exportable, and even Israelis sometimes feel that the system is declining as industrial expansion and technological advancement take its place. Yet perhaps this is a mistaken point of view. The kibbutz was a major factor in the founding of the State and even today it makes a major contribution. The founders of new settlements, who work on the kibbutz as part of Army service, accept the same pioneering values and, to a great extent, adopt the same principles, as the early settlers. The established kibbutzim have shown a capacity for adjustment, a widening of their activities and traditions, which keeps them from stagnating or becoming mere relics of a past era.

Fundamentally, a kibbutz is nothing more than a large farming settlement where people live and work as a voluntary group for the benefit of all. The activities are basically agricultural, often associated with the reclamation of the land. Paid labour is contrary to kibbutz principles—all members are equal and are entitled to equal shares of the results of the enterprise. Ownership and responsibility are collective, activities are communal. It is this rejection of material values that attracts so many young people who come not to join the kibbutz but to stay for a time and share its existence. Some of the more popular kibbutzim resemble a kind of international youth club at the height of the holiday season and, although very few actually become permanent members, most find it a rewarding experience.

The life is disciplined but informal and the principle of collective responsibility means that the settlement is run on entirely democratic lines and decisions are taken by vote. As the kibbutz's survival is assured, its members can turn their attention to the quality of life within it. More houses, perhaps, can be built, providing greater privacy; more money spent on cultural amenities, and so on. And security is life-long, even those no longer fit for the more demanding jobs being able to 'retire' either partly or wholly, though most people continue to make some work contribution.

Does this all sound very idealistic? Perhaps it does, but then the kibbutz is an ideal, and in order to understand how it came about, it is necessary to go back to the origins of Zionism. In the nineteenth century, at a time when anti-semitism was old and socialism young, the Zionist pioneers who came to the Holy Land, came to build a Jewish homeland based on social justice and independence. They believed, as Theodor Herzl believed, that the Jews had been deprived not only of their ancient homeland, but also of their ability to survive in it. The Jews in the Diaspora had become rootless and disengaged from normal society, restricted to performing menial or clerical functions, at best a group of itinerant traders.

Nation-building therefore had to be coupled with creative skills of all kinds, agricultural skills above all else. For centuries the Jew in the Diaspora had been divorced from the land. His ancestors had been pastoral herdsmen and the Jewish festivals bear testimony to the rural society, as indeed does the Bible, but in exile, Jews had confined themselves to performing symbolic actions which commemorated planting or harvest times.

The pioneers realized that independence and self-reliance were synonymous concepts, that nation-building entailed building a love for the land and acceptance of the dignity of labour. This dovetailed with the other ideal, that of socialism, in believing that exploitation of one man by another was unacceptable.

Such concepts led to the establishment of the first kibbutz and while the methods used were later modified and the kibbutz structure of today evolved over decades, they remain the basic principles. Co-operative farming, kibbutz style, became a hallmark of the Jewish State.

One man who contributed many of these ideas was Aaron David Gordon, whose work *Philosophy of Labour* gave the kibbutz its ideological background. Born in Russia in 1857, Gordon died in Palestine in 1922 and his theories deeply influenced his colleagues and contemporaries. He believed in the change of the individual before the transformation or rebirth of the State, in the development of man as a social being and the evolvement of personal responsibility, before a material socialist revolution. He realized that the rootless Jew could achieve harmonious creativity through physical labour on the land, which would become a new identification with nature and represent revival of social and national awareness. Gordon's belief in the dignity of labour and the personality deeply affected the Jewish labour movement.

Many others influenced the early settlers, including the great Martin Buber. All were concerned with ending exploitation and injustice. The kibbutz movement was the tool perfected to create the rebirth of an old nation and people by providing enthusiasm and a practical basis for a socialist way of life.

The kibbutz became an instrument of Jewish settlement of Palestine. The Jewish National Fund acquired land, which it handed over for cultivation to small groups of young people who lived and worked together, creating homes and fields on previously barren soil. The determination and devotion of the pioneers and the creation of the kibbutz has become synonymous with the establishment of the State of Israel and in many ways represents the greatest ideals of Zionism.

The kibbutz has been labelled the only true socialist experience of our time. It has become the subject of research for sociologists, political scientists, economists, and for Israel, was the breeding ground for its first generations of leaders in politics, the defence forces, the arts and sciences.

The first kibbutz was founded in 1909 in the Jordan Valley, south of Lake Kinneret. The founders were a dozen teenagers, ten boys and two girls, who were part of the wave of immigrants of the Second Aliyah. Eager, dedicated, zealous, they lacked formal training and decided that they stood a better chance of survival as a group rather than as individuals. They could have worked as farm hands on established Jewish farms, for the first settlements were villages along traditional lines, with individual ownership, but this was not what they wanted. Degania, the first kibbutz, was just that, a kibbutz, with the young people sharing the hazards and the rewards of collective farming.

The youngsters came from Eastern Europe from middle-class families. They were imbued with Zionist ideals and believed in the Tolstoyan philosophy of self-labour. The land they were given belonged to the Jewish National Fund, all 750 acres of it. The land was in fact swamp, unproductive and malaria-infested and open to Arab raids. The young people worked with great devotion; they cleared the undergrowth, dug ditches, moved rocks and boulders, planted eucalyptus trees and, after two years, had cleared and cultivated several hundred acres of land—a tremendous achievement.

Seventy-five years after its beginnings, Degania is a settlement with farmlands and orchards, a major dairy herd, stone houses, gardens, a school and museum and, of course, its communal facilities. The swamps have disappeared and Degania is one of a series of settlements in the Jordan valley, whose combined plantations stretch for miles around.

The success of Degania, and its failures, established the kibbutz as a mode of life. The original idea, that members should contribute their labour and in return receive not wages, but services of the kind for which payment is extracted in other societies, has remained. Kibbutz members are equal shareholders by virtue of their labour in an enterprise which gives them shelter and food and other services, such as care and schooling for their children, medical attention, entertainment, clothing. They also receive social security when ill or too old to work. But they receive nothing except the clothes they wear, if they leave.

Their work goes into the communal enterprise as their lifelong investment. It develops and extends that enterprise and in return, the members benefit. Thus food consumed in a new kibbutz, where members still live in tents or wooden huts, will be frugal. Items such as fresh fruit and vegetables which are accepted as an ordinary, essential part of everyday menus, are luxuries in new kibbutzim. Yet established kibbutzim offer a life not so very different to that on any privately-owned commercial unit whose workers live in modern homes, own a radio, eat well and work regular hours.

In time as Kibbutz life passes through these stages of development, the new kibbutzim will also offer more to their members. As their collective efforts pay off, the 'surplus' of their labour is ploughed back, so their individual lot improves. But it improves equally for all the members. There are no personal possessions. Inheritance or, in the decades after the end of the Second World War and the holocaust, restitution payments, go to the common kibbutz fund. Money is not used inside the kibbutz.

It is not possible to buy kibbutz membership either with money or qualifications. One has to be accepted as a member, either as a founding member when a settlement gets under way, in which case one is presumably young, single and healthy, or one can apply for membership in an existing kibbutz again preferably while one is young, single and healthy. The usual rule is a year's apprenticeship, before a decision on acceptance is taken. Any member can leave at any time, but naturally a step such as this is not taken lightly.

The structure of a kibbutz is essentially democratic. There is a type of 'parliament', the general assembly in which each member has a vote and where a simple majority is the basis of decision. The general assembly is convened when required and concerns itself with all important issues of the community. Each year the executive is elected. The general secretary is the main appointment, a kind of mayor or perhaps prime minister. In addition there is a treasurer, a technical secretary, another in charge of agriculture and finally the person detailed to take charge of external relations, that is to say, of transactions of buying and selling, and as linkman with the various authorities. These persons constitute a cabinet, which is newly elected each year, in an effort to stop the establishment of bureaucrats.

In addition, specialist committees are elected to assist the executive secretariat. The 'government' of the kibbutz is carried on by these committees, whose membership may include as many as one-third of the total of members at any one time. There is usually a committee on economics and planning, others on housing, on man-power, spots, entertainment, education.

The kibbutz does not distribute wages or dividends. The members aim for a standard of living, which at the beginning is nothing except the bare essentials of life; later the style is appropriate to total income. Thus in the pioneer days a routine had become established. Once land had been allocated to a group of chaverim, the group would arrive early one morning, complete with prefabricated material. The first job would have been the construction of a fence and the watchtower. A searchlight would instantly be installed in the tower, worked by a generator. Thus by nightfall primitive sleeping quarters would be ready and could be guarded against Arab attackers.

The spirit of self-reliance engendered by the pioneers is kept alive as far as is possible in more affluent and secure periods. The principle of no privileges is applied in all kibbutzim. Private property, like hired labour, has no room in a kibbutz. Everything is shared, which means that the woman is no longer tied to the traditional role of housewife and nursemaid. There are single and married quarters of a type befitting the level of collective income. Members eat together, send their clothes to the kibbutz laundry, the washing up is done by those detailed for the job, whilst child-rearing or teaching is handled by others. Most work is done on a collective basis in rotation.

Economic decisions concerning surplus funds are made by the general assembly. For instance, a decision may revolve around using available funds for a new shower or for additional theatre tickets for everyone during the year. Such points are discussed thoroughly before the vote is taken.

There are no private households as such. Man and wife live in their room or rooms and they see their children regularly. In some kibbutzim the children also sleep in the same quarters as their parents. It is more usual for children to stay with their peer groups in the children's houses. No expense is spared in any kibbutz as far as the children are concerned. They are the community's most precious possessions and are treated as such. The parent-child relationship in the kibbutzim has also been the subject of a good deal of study by researchers. There is no doubt that the children do not suffer from deprivation and receive tremendous parental love and affection, while their physical care and education is in the hands of specialists from the day they are born. The needs of the children, their welfare, education, security is of vital importance to the kibbutz ideal and Zionist aspiration. The children's houses are built in the centre of the settlement for greater security.

The concept of equality means that a doctor ranks equal with the tractor driver or shepherd. (It also means that the shepherd or tractor driver can have as many degrees as the doctor.) The kibbutzim are well-known for their high standards of cultural life, both in music and the arts. Talented members are educated at the expense of the community and membership is not forfeited when they leave to serve as diplomats, politicians or in any other capacity.

Indeed, service to the community is expected of a kibbutznik and, is determined without material considerations independent of the size of income. The kibbutz membership affords security of a kind not available to the Western capitalist society, which of course also prevails in urban Israel.

It is essential to understand the psychology of a kibbutznik in order to understand his way of life. The bourgois values of material advancement are not kibbutz standards. Physical labour is not denigrated, and intellectuals rate manual work as highly as intellectual output. In particular, collective aims and achievements take precedence over personal ambition. The kibbutz provides emotional and physical security, but it also demands loss of privacy. Introverts or egotistic temperaments cannot easily accept this. In the early days of the kibbutzim, pooled experience and pooled ownership was sometimes taken to extremes, but as members matured, married and had families, some of the extremism was found unworkable. Debates concerning greater privacy, greater parental control over children and similar issues still form part of the kibbutz scene, although many ideas have stabilized and the kibbutz is long past the experimental stage.

The community has the feel of the extended family. Parents of members are accepted in the kibbutzim, and live separately, having often bought their way into the parent block through giving up an urban flat or pension. Second and third generation offspring can and do opt for kibbutz life and it is possible for parents to see their children's children grow up around them — something rarely experienced in an urban society whose modern tendency is that of scattering families, not gathering them together.

There is, of course, another side to the picture. The system does not suit everyone. Some kibbutzniks leave the land as they approach middle age, or children born on a kibbutz choose urban life when they grow up. The system attracts not only the idealist, but also the perpetually immature, the person who cannot easily accept responsibility, the man or woman who lacks inner resources or who looks for easy solutions to deepseated personal problems. One of the reasons why one year's probation is considered essential is because kibbutzniks realize that there can be many reasons which may lead someone towards the kibbutz and that not all reasons are good ones.

For young people, the kibbutz has the unrivalled attraction of adventure, the same sort of attraction that made youngsters work their passage on freighters or in a past era, join the Foreign Legion. Pioneer work in the Negev is exciting and challenging, offering hardship, danger and the reward of achievement.

The kibbutz is linked with a political movement or to a lesser extent religious organization. Being a radical social experiment, the kibbutz is a practical expression of socialistic theory, a physical expression of socialism. Politics are important in the life of the kibbutzim. Theories and beliefs differ from one group to another. Most kibbutzim are affiliated to the socialist parties, some to the labour-religious party.

Six of the movements are grouped together since 1963 in a Federation of the Kibbutz Movements. The Federation is the umbrella organization for almost all kibbutzim and committees cover every aspect of kibbutz life. The individual movements continue with their own separate committee work. Thus the Federation's committee on economic affairs handles land, water, housing, planning, new settlements, marketing budgets and similar items, representing the kibbutzim for authorities such as the Jewish Agency or government departments.

There is an association of kibbutz industries, an inter-kibbutz training unit for management and administration, a research committee which looks at various aspects of kibbutz life. Other units deal with health and education. An inter-kibbutz committee deals with the absorption of newcomers and administers a network of world-wide offices advising would-be immigrants on land settlement. The Federation adds to the cultural activities of the kibbutz movements themselves, having established a kibbutz stage, literary circles a chamber orchestra and a central dancing group.

The rigidity of the social framework of the kibbutz led to another form of collective farming, named the moshav. In this community, there are individual households but collective work on the fields and in purchasing and marketing. In addition, people own equal portions of land, which they farm for their private gain. The moshav is more flexible and less demanding on the individual and thus has the greater appeal to immigrants who want to live on the land.

The kibbutz and moshav population is increasing, despite the complaint that the austerity and self-denial demanded do not appeal to newcomers. In 1922 the kibbutz population numbered 939 but by 1971 had reached 86,300. There are around 250 kibbutzim which accounts for about one-third of the country's rural population and new kibbutzim are still being established. The system has proved an economic success. The kibbutz population is three and a half per cent of Israel's population, but produces thirty per cent of agricultural and seven per cent of industrial output. Kibbutz agriculture is on par with that of the developed countries, milk production is at the US level and cotton yields are the highest in the world. During the past decade, the kibbutz has accepted industrial production as part of its programme and in future the major part of the kibbutz income will be derived from industry, a process requiring adjustment in approach and kibbutz philosophy, which in the beginning was essentially one of return to the land. New industries include textiles, consumer products, food, electronics, furniture, chemicals.

The kibbutzim were breeding grounds for Israel's élite and so played a part in the country's early development out of proportion to the number or size of the kibbutz population. With new immigrants working on the land in more conventional settlements, and with the growth of the urban centres and their own élite, the role of the kibbutzim in this respect is declining.

But it is unlikely to decline in the economic sense. The diversification into industry is important, representing a new phase in kibbutz development and that of the country, in general. The return to the Land was the basic idea of the kibbutz movement. But in a small country such as Israel, proximity to urban markets, availability of managerial skills and good teamwork, offer a natural stimulus to improve the economic viability of a kibbutz project by extending efforts to industry. In this way, industrialization does not break up social patterns, as it did in the European industrial society, but strengthens established organizations. A new partnership between the kibbutz and private investors must of course develop, forcing a new assessment of kibbutz values upon the kibbutznik. It must be a new stress added to those inherent in the system, that of balancing the ideal of sharing against that of desire for private experience.

The success of the system is seen in the rebirth of Jewish life on the land, in the blossoming of a country with few arable resources, by creating a pattern of life for communities which is desirable from the point of view of the state, the economy and the individual. The kibbutz combines rural living with modern technology. It has already a tradition of its own, but tradition is not the most powerful factor. Adaptation and modification are still essential, if the kibbutzim are to survive.

Essentially, the kibbutz represents old relationships in a new environment, the interaction of community, family and the individual. For those who choose to remain as kibbutzniks, the new social order provides security through familiarity with the same people and the shared experiences with these people, in work and recreation. It is a life-style that calls for imagination combined with practicality. It has also succeeded in combining tradition with something completely new.

Index

Abraham, 10, 94, 109, 145
Abu Ghosh, 95
Acre, 26–27, 76 et. seq.
Aeolia Capitolina, 21, 55, 66
Afula, 120
El Aksa, 57, 61
Alexander, 15, 16
Alexandria, 16
Anastasis, 22, 56
Antiochus Epiphanes, 16, 52
Antonia, 19, 55
Arad, 88, 141
El Arish, 157
Ashdod, 12, 88
Ashkelon, 12, 76 et seq.
Assyrians, 9, 14, 51, 114
Avdat, 154

Bab El Wad, 95
Babylon, 15, 51
Babylonian Exile, 15, 51
Baghdad, 25, 57
Bahai Sect, 77, 80
Balfour, 31
Banias, 111, 160
Bat Yam, 127
Baybars, 26, 59
Bedouin, 24, 28, 66, 98, et seq.
Beersheba, 10, 42 et seq.
Belvoir, 117
Beth El, 109
Bethlehem, 19, 22, 28, 96, et seq.
Beth Shean, 16, 118
Byzantine Empire, 22, 55

Calvary, 60

Capernaum, 116
Cesarea, 9, 10, 12
Citadel, 69, 70
Church of the Holy Sepulchre, 26, 55
Church of the Nativity, 28
Constantine, 22, 55, 57, 97
Constantinople, 27, 56, 61, 62
Crusaders, 24, 25, 58 et seq.
Cyrus, 15, 51

Damascus Gate, 61, 66, 70
David, 12, 50, 69, 75, 100
Dead Sea, 10, 17, 96 et seq.
Dionysus, 16
Dome of the Rock, 58, 61
Dormition, 63, 74
Druze, 43, 44, 82, 117
Dung Gate, 69

Egypt, 9, 10, 11, 13, 15, 16, 24, 57, 114, 143
Eilat, 151 et seq.
Elija, 79
Ein Gedi, 102
Ein Gev, 115
Ein Hod, 82
Ein Kerem, 64

Galilee, 19, 20, 25, 72, 44, 111 et seq.
Garden Tomb, 67
Gaza, 12, 160
Gehenna, 49, 59
Gihon, 68, 74
Gilboa, 12, 118
Golan, 44, 111, 159
Goliath, 12

174 *Israel*

Golgotha, 55, 66
Greece, 16

Hadrian, 55, 56
Haganh, 32, 80
Haifa, 25, 79 *et seq.*
Har Hazikaron, 73
Hazor, 13, 113
Hebrews, 10
Hebron, 10, 25, 96, 99 *et seq.*
Herod, 19, 52, 61, 69 *et seq.*
Herodian, 99
Herzl, 30–31, 73, 80
Herzlia, 86, 127
Hezekiah, 74
Horns of Hattin, 26, 117
Hoveve Zion, 24
Hula Valley, 111 *et seq.*
Hyksos, 10

Isaac, 10
Isaiah, 51
Islam, 23, 24, 26 *et seq.*

Jaffa, 16, 25–26, 133–137
Jaffa Gate, 19, 55, 61, 63 *et seq.*
Jericho, 96, 103 *et seq.*
Jeroboam, 13
Jerusalem, 12, 13, 14 *et seq.*
Jezreel Valley, 32, 111, 118
Jordan, 11, 20, 120 *et seq.*
Jove, 16
Judah, 13, 14, 52
Judea, 20, 65, 94 *et seq.*
Judges, 11

Kafr Kana, 122
Karaites, 43
Kidron Valley, 22, 44, 59, 68
Kiryat Shmona, 112
Kiryat Yearim, 95
Knesset, 36, 43, 64
Knights Hospitallers, 25, 58
Knights Templars, 25, 58, 79
Kochba, 21, 55

Land, The, 23, 36
Latrun, 95
Lion's Gate, 59

Machnei Yehuda, 65
Machpela, 96, 101
Majd El Shams, 160
Mamelukes, 26, 28, 60
Mandate, 31
Masada, 21, 147
Mar Saba, 22, 98
Mea Shearim, 63, 65
Mecca, 23, 153
Medina, 23
Mediterranean, 9, 12, 99, 111
Megiddo, 13, 14, 123
Messiah, 20, 65, 117
Mitla, 157
Mons Gaudii, 110
Montfort, 117
Moses, 10, 11
Mosque of Omar, 57
Mount of Beatitudes, 116
Mount Carmel, 79, 80
Mount Ebal, 106
Mount Gerizim, 106
Mount Hermon, 111, 160
Mount Moriah, 57
Mount of Olives, 22, 67, 68, 96
Mount Tabor, 120
Mount Zion, 62, 74, 75

Nablus, 106
Nahariya, 119
Napoleon, 27, 77
Natanya, 86
Nazareth, 22, 121
Negev, 32, 141 *et seq.*

October War, 45
Omar, 23, 24, 56, 57
Ottomans, 27, 77, 160

Palestine, 16, 21, 23 *et seq.*
Petah Tikva, 30
Pharisees, 17, 20
Philistines, 12, 88, 160
Phoenicia, 9, 76
Pompey, 19, 52

Rachel's Tomb, 96
Ramallah, 94, 95, 109
Ramat Aviv, 135
Ramla, 95

Ras Muhamed, 159
Red Sea, 25, 159
Rehoboam, 13
Rehovot, 87
Richard II, 26, 60, 77
Rishon-le-Zion, 30, 87
Rome, 20, 21, 52, 55, 84
Rosh Pinna, 30, 112

Saduccees, 19
Safed, 28, 111, 114
Saladin, 26, 60, 77
Samaria, 14, 94 *et seq.*
Saul, 12
Sdom, 149
Second Temple, 84
Seljuks, 24, 58
Shar Hagai, 95
Sharm El Sheikh, 159
Shechem, 106, 109
Shiloh, 12, 22, 109
Shivta, 154
Siloam, 74
Sinai, 11, 44, 141, 157 *et seq.*
Six Day War, 14
Solomons Pools, 94
St. Stephen's Gate, 73

Suleiman the Magnificent, 61
Suez, 141, 157

Taghba, 116
Talmud, 39, 45
Tel Aviv, 65, 86, 126 *et seq.*
Temple, The, 50, 55, 62, 115
Tiberias, 21, 111, 114, 159
Timna, 147, 150
Tiran, 159
Torah, 20, 65
Turks, 26

Umayyads, 24, 28
U.N., 45, 66

Weizmann, 31, 63, 86
West Bank, 44, 94
Western Wall, 55, 62, 70, 96

Yafo, 126, 133, 137 *et seq.*
Yarkon, 127
Yavneh, 88
Yotvata, 151

Zealots, 21, 99
Zionism, 28 *et seq.*

DS
107.4
L313
1916

Larsen, Elaine.
Israel

DATE			

DRAUGHON'S COLLEGE
SAVANNAH

South University
709 Mall Blvd
Savannah, GA 31406

© THE BAKER & TAYLOR CO.